Bert J Wellman

The legal Revolution of 1902

Bert J Wellman

The legal Revolution of 1902

ISBN/EAN: 9783743322158

Manufactured in Europe, USA, Canada, Australia, Japa

Cover: Foto ©ninafisch / pixelio.de

Manufactured and distributed by brebook publishing software (www.brebook.com)

Bert J Wellman

The legal Revolution of 1902

Price 25 Cents

The Co=opolitan

By Zebina Forbush

A STORY OF THE CO-OPERATIVE
COMMONWEALTH OF IDAHO.

Charles H. Kerr & Company, Publishers
56 FIFTH AVENUE, CHICAGO

BANCROFT LIBRARY

THE O-OPOLITAN

A Story of the Co-operative Commonwealth of Idaho.

BY
ZEBINA FORBUSH.

"'Tis coming up the Steep of Time
And this old World is growing brighter."
—*Gerald Massey.*

CHICAGO:
CHARLES H. KERR & COMPANY.
1898.

Copyright 1898
By Charles H. Kerr & Company.

Library of Progress. No. 26. Quarterly $1.00 a year. February, 1898.
Entered at the Postoffice, Chicago, as second-class matter.

PREFACE.

This volume is given to the public without other excuse than the simple fact that it has been written. If it is read it may do some good, but in any event it cannot do injury. If it is not read the hour which knew it will pass with it, and countless hours, like waves in Time's ocean, will roll on multitudinously, with their burdens of good and evil, and pass also.

Because the writer believed he had a thought to express, which, if heeded, would help, in some slight degree, to right human wrongs, he ventured to offer it in this form. He had discovered by experience that no radical and permanent reform can be successfully effected without the consent of what are called "the substantial business interests" of the established system.

He has also observed that the system now in operation is constantly undergoing changes, and that our predecessors in its control, of a quarter of a century ago, would scarcely recognize the system by which we live to-day. These changes have been accomplished through evolution only. Numbers count for nothing. Millions submit readily to the will of one.

Education counts for everything, and if we had been taught that to stand on our heads an hour a day was essential to salvation most of us would observe that form without question. Some, however, are superior to error and are strong enough to be and to do right. But these are scattered. They argue with their unthinking neighbors and are ridiculed for their pains. Such methods never did succeed and the world is as much out of gear with righteousness to-day as it was in the dark ages.

This is the trouble with political Co-operation. It cannot succeed except in a very slight measure. Why? Because industrial and commercial education are against it. Because the Industrial System is against it. Because the great, the powerful and strong are against it. Political Co-operation has no money with which to compete with the competitive system. Righteousness without money is a will-o'-the-wisp as against Mephisto, with millions in the competitive system.

Co-operation must enter the lists with means and weapons similar to its opponents, or else it will fail. Therefore the writer proposes that the profits of co-operation be matched against the profits of competition, and if co-operation can "win out" then the profit system is dead.

Let us raise the cry of Industrial Co-operation against Industrial Competition, and then go to work. When we are strong enough we will do what Industrial Competition in the form of corporations and syndicates has done. We will become political. Industrially we can grow as all industrial institutions have, and when we are grown to a magnitude which forces recognition, the world is ours and again belongs, not to a few, but to all of us.

This little volume is designed to show, in part, what an opportunity we have to plant the flag of Industrial Co-operation on American soil and defend it as it cannot be defended in any other country.

Yours Fraternally,

THE AUTHOR.

THE CO-OPOLITAN.

CHAPTER I.

THE YEAR 1897.

During the entire existence of the great American republic no year seemed more hopeless to the masses of its people than the year 1897.

It is true that the dark hours of conflict, when separation from Great Britain was sought at the cannon's mouth, and later, when civil strife nearly rent the nation in twain, seemed, to superficial observers, to be more fraught with danger.

But the problems of those times could be and were readily understood. Success to the arms of the patriots, in the one case, and the Unionists in the other, was a simple solution, although distressing in its pursuit and difficult of achievement.

But this year was one which was the culmination of many years of singular abundance, blessed by nature in almost every conceivable way, and yet by a strange contradiction of circumstances full of sorrow, distress, hunger and poverty.

The wealth of this, the richest country in the world, was made valueless by reason of the belief on the part of its people that it must borrow the right to use that wealth from other nations. The supplies of food, clothing and materials of all kinds were vast, and yet the inhabitants for some cause were not able to obtain them, although their needs were great. There were now a few rich and many—very many—extremely poor.

It was this strange, contradictory, confusing and incomprehensible condition which made men hopeless. Where to look for help, what to do, the cause, the consequence, the evil and the remedy, were all subjects of agitation and deep concern. Everybody except those few who were satisfied with any condition which did not disturb their own happiness, had views on these subjects and had conceived of some remedy. And the multiplicity of these views and the innumerable varieties of remedies proposed, seemed to aggravate the general despair and produce an increasing paralysis of action.

It was in January of that dismal year that I found myself in the great city of Chicago. I, too, had been affected by the universal depreciation of property, so that a fortune of fifty thousand dollars, which I had inherited from my parents, was now dubiously estimated to have dwindled to something like ten thousand dollars. I knew it was not my fault.

Bank stocks, railroad stocks and mining stocks, represented the bulk of my poor, deceased father's savings and investments.

Much of this could not attract buyers at any price. Some could not be given away. The rest was convertible into gold at a few cents on the dollar.

But I was too young, being only twenty-five years of age, to become despondent over the loss of money, and I had traveled so extensively about my own country and seen its countless opportunities that I felt a certain elation in the prospect of building up a fortune of my own.

So that, although a stranger in Chicago, with no friends nearer than Massachusetts, and without the smallest idea of a plan for the future, I yet had a firm belief in God, man, my country and myself.

I did not even doubt the system which had robbed me of my fortune, and was inclined to look upon all who denounced it as hostile to the best interests of mankind.

My education was, in a large measure, responsible for this. Born in Salem, Massachusetts, one of the oldest, sleepiest and most conservative of American cities, educated in her schools and in one of the staid old colleges, for which New England was justly famous, how could I have imbibed anything but ancient, sleepy and conservative theories of political economy, and fine, staid and somewhat musty notions of the end and purpose of man?

It is true that my extensive travels had broadened me somewhat mentally. They had taught me the value of individual men and had rather obliterated sectional pride, which I was willing to confess was the besetting sin of the average New Englander; they had made me acquainted with manners and customs and had produced in me a capability of adjusting myself to delicate situations.

But this sort of breadth, while excellent and serviceable, did not render me tolerant of ideas which were at variance with those commonly accepted. My distinguishing characteristic, on which I prided myself not a little, was an almost encyclopedic knowledge of the history and resources of my own country. I mention this particularly now, because I had occasion, later on, to turn my knowledge to a very useful purpose.

I was inclined to remain in Chicago. There was no reason for it which I had defined to myself, and I really believe that, of all the dismal places I had ever seen, Chicago was the most dismal at that time. I did not have any occupation, attraction or hope to keep me in this maelstrom of the human ocean.

I did not like it. I had no friends in it. I did not seem to find companions. Indeed, I was happy in being alone, and enjoyed a certain discontent, which was productive of thoughtfulness, and which set me to expressing my thoughts on paper.

Governed by an instinctive prudence, which is characteristic of the New England mind, I had selected a room in a respectable private house, where there were also two other roomers, and took my meals at a neighboring restaurant.

CHAPTER II.

JOHN THOMPSON—CO-OPERATION

One day after I had been settled in Chicago for, perhaps, two or three weeks, the sun shone so brightly and the weather was so mild that I was tempted to stroll out, on so exceptional an occasion for Chicago, into the suburbs of the great city. As I wandered along aimlessly, watching the gay sleighing parties, I saw one of the young men who roomed in the same house coming toward me from the opposite direction.

I had become so far acquainted with him as to have learned that his name was Thompson, and had overheard some of his conversation with companions who called at his room. What I had heard and seen did not impress me favorably. He seemed to entertain and express views of an economic nature which were not in accord with my New England notions, and I was disposed to avoid him. My first impulse, in fact, was to cross this street and continue my way alone. Before I could do this, however, Thompson hailed me with a cheerful, courteous and familiar "How do you do?" So cordial, good-natured and attractive seemed his manner, devoid of all affectation or obtrusiveness, that I stopped, returned his salutation and suddenly became conscious of a desire to have company in my walk. So I asked him which way he was bound, and on his replying that he was simply taking a stroll we both turned into a side street, and continuing the walk together entered into conversation.

Thompson was really a remarkable looking man. I marveled, as I walked along with him, that I had not noticed this in the two weeks that we had roomed in the same house, but probably it was because we saw each other only once in awhile in the hallway as we passed. I now observed that he was a man fully six feet tall, erect and powerfully built, with a thoughtful, clean-shaven face, strong features and great earnest, commanding eyes. Indeed it seemed to me that I never had seen such eyes before. One felt that they belonged to a master and that this man was a natural leader of his kind. But I then thought, and afterward learned, that he was not only a leader but a thinker Such a man could, if his heart was enlisted in any cause, sacrifice not merely life, but, if need be, reputation for the good cause in which he believed.

"I have thought, Mr. Braden," said he, as we sauntered along together, "that you might be interested in a little project some of us have to improve the condition of the masses of our people. Have you ever studied the question of co-operation?"

"No, sir," said I. "I have never studied the question of co-operation. I presume you mean, sir, co-operation among laborers. But while I have not studied it I must admit that I have little sympathy with the theory. It is not practicable and all attempts which I have observed have failed."

"Pardon me, Mr. Braden," returned my companion. "I feel that you have not observed the noble and very successful co-operative enterprises which flourish throughout Europe and to some extent in the United States at this time. The truth is, co-operation has proven to be and is strikingly practicable. In the United Kingdom of Great Britain and Ireland $60,000,000.00 and more constitutes the accumulated capital of co-operative societies and on the continent of Europe the capital involved is much greater."

It is not my purpose to detail our discussion of this subject. Suffice it to say that nearly the whole day was spent in each other's society. Although by no means convinced at the close of the day that Thompson was correct in his views, I found myself deeply interested. I resolved to study the subject and study it fairly.

The project which my new acquaintance outlined was one which I at once pronounced visionary. It was, he said, the design of certain gentlemen, some of whom lived in

Chicago, to organize what they called the Co-operative Commonwealth. These gentlemen had decided to induce laboring men and other persons who might be willing to associate themselves in the work to form co-operative societies and to colonize them in some one state, so that, in process of time, they would outvote the devotees of the old system. When this desired result was achieved, they made no doubt that the Co-operative Commonwealth would be established and present to the entire world an example of prosperity which would rouse an unquenchable spirit of emulation. I could not forbear to sneer at the plan when it was explained, but when I saw how serious Thompson was, and looking into his face felt the impression of his strong character, I was inclined to think about it and began, involuntarily, to picture to myself an ideal of the Co-operative Commonwealth.

That day Thompson and I were together much of the time and went to the public library, at his suggestion, to prove some of his statements, the correctness of which I had disputed. I was obliged to admit, when we parted, that he had made no mistake, and this satisfied me that he was an authority on social and economic questions.

This man was, at the time when our meeting and conversation occurred, about thirty-five years of age. He was an Englishman by birth, but came to this country when only three years of age with his parents, and settled in Red Bluff, California, where his mother died shortly after. When about fifteen he removed with his father to a mining town in Nevada, where the father speedily acquired a fortune in mercantile pursuits and in some fortunate speculations in mining stocks. The son was impatient of restraint as a boy, ran away from home, and visited nearly all the mining camps in the west, followed every excitement, became a skillful miner and acquired an immense fund of useful and curious information.

When about thirty he drifted to Chicago and worked at a variety of occupations, being a master of many, but never rose above the station of a journeyman. This was due to the fact that he worked only that he might obtain money to procure books, principally on questions of political economy, and had no aspiration to follow any life but that of a student. One day when he had been in the city for some years he saw his father, now an old man, in the crowd on State street. He had lost all trace of him many years before, and once in his wanderings he had gone to the Nevada mining town where he last saw him, and had found the town deserted except by two old men, who could give him no information as to where his father had gone. They simply knew that when he went away he was accounted one of the wealthiest men in the camp. Now, meeting him on the street of the great city, he observed that he seemed to have about him every indication of wealth and position. He spoke to him, calling him father, and was recognized by the old gentleman, but with some difficulty. Events following were sufficiently interesting.

Thompson was taken to his father's palatial residence on the Wisconsin lake shore, not far from Chicago, and for a while lived in great luxury. But this was ill suited to his character and entirely at variance with the habits he had formed during his rough western life. He became restless, and made numerous trips to the city, where he spent his time in the libraries and among his books. His father, who was in truth very wealthy, usually went south in the winter and was in Florida at that time. On the day when I met the son he designed to take the evening train for his father's southern home, intending to go from there to Arizona, where the old gentleman has some mining interests, but expecting to return to Chicago in March.

When he parted with me that afternoon he urged me to pursue certain economic lines of inquiry, advising me what books to read, and requesting me to give him my views on co-operation when he should next meet me. This I promised to do, and when we went our several ways I found myself looking at the world with new eyes, but with a feeling that I was getting on rather too familiar terms with a number of political heresies.

CHAPTER III.

A MEETING OF THE CO-OPERATIVE COMMONWEALTH—COMMITTEE APPOINTED TO VISIT IDAHO.

After the introduction of the subject to my notice, in the manner described in the foregoing pages, I spent nearly all of my time for at least a month in the study of such books as had been suggested to me, treating upon the condition of labor in what is ordinarily called the Christian world. I was engaged in this occupation when Thompson returned from his trip to the South and West. To say that I had become convinced that Thompson's plan of co-operation and the establishment of a Co-operative Commonwealth was practicable would not be true, but in all my researches I had kept his plan in mind and confessed that I was anxious to see it put into practice.

I was not convinced by any means that it would succeed, but I wanted to observe its workings and believed that it could do no evil. Therefore when I again met Thompson about the middle of March, I made haste to assure him that I was prepared to approve his theories and desirous of taking some part in the experiment which I hoped would be tried. Upon learning this, Thompson informed me that he was already a member of the Co-operative Commonwealth, that a meeting of some of the most influential projectors would be held that evening, and that he would like to have me present. I readily accepted the invitation and at the appointed time and place met him that evening, and together we went to the meeting.

I was quite surprised upon entering the little hall where his friends had assembled to find myself in the midst of well-dressed, refined, intellectual and apparently practical men. Thompson introduced me to a number of these as a friend who was interested in the Co-operative Commonwealth and who would, as he thought, contribute to its success.

Although I felt that this recommendation of me was premature, yet I made no objection to it, because I preferred to accept the cordial reception which his introduction seemed to procure for me. We spent about half-an hour in conversation on subjects involving the co-operative idea. I had little to say, personally, but rather confined myself to asking questions until the meeting was called to order. But from what was told me in answer to my questions I was deeply impressed by the apparent sincerity and general benevolence which pervaded the assemblage.

I confess that I rather expected to find a somewhat motley crowd of men, with wild staring eyes, shaggy, unkempt heads and beards, indulging with furious gestures and loud voices in bitter and irrational denunciation of the government and public institutions of my country.

Instead of that these men were as sleek, as mild, as quiet and gentlemanly as an equal number of bank presidents might be. Perhaps more so. At any rate, I have seen bank presidents and directors congregate together in less orderly conventions and have heard from them far more expressions of contempt for our government and its laws than these men uttered. The truth was that the gentlemen whom I now had the honor to meet were more fervently patriotic than any similar assemblage I had ever seen. Men who come together in the name of a church, a party, a bank, a business enterprise or even a particular charity, are not prone to hold country above all other objects. But these men, gathering in the name of humanity, held their country to be, by reason of its location, character, condition and opportunities, the most suitable field for whatever was and is best in the human race.

When the meeting opened Thompson, who was evidently held in great esteem, assumed the position of presiding officer. He began with a brief statement of its purposes.

"Gentlemen," said he, "this meeting is called for a purpose with which you are doubtless all familiar. Lest there should be persons among you, however, who are not fully informed, I deem it proper to make a brief statement at this time. The present business and financial depression, spreading as it does throughout most of Christendom, has produced a feeling of unrest among those classes of people who feel it most. This unrest is admitted by all who have eyes with which to observe, and minds with which to analyze, to be fraught with danger. It threatens our security, it threatens our homes, it threatens morals and religion, it threatens the stability of our institutions, the existence of the republic and the durability of Christian civilization.

"It is the protest of blind Samson against the exactions of the Philistines. It is the human heart overflowing with bitterness at the injustice of men and classes. Ere the pillars of the temple tremble and the walls of the temple fall upon us, we offer a remedy and ask that it be applied. In justice to ourselves, let me say, that we propose this remedy experimentally. We do not, by any means, know whether the human system is capable of receiving it, but we are absolutely certain that it can do no injury. We are also equally certain that the attempt to apply it will improve the condition of those who actively participate in our plan. I ought also to say that if our remedy is accepted and applied with earnestness and intelligence it will not fail.

"There are in the American states over 200,000 voters who believe that the true theory of economics is that the machinery of production belongs to the people in common. These are convinced that in the theory so expressed lies the remedy for those economic evils which produce the extremes of great poverty and great wealth. They are also ready to participate in some concerted movement which will enable them to establish a Co-operative Commonwealth in one of our American states. Our plan is to direct all those who believe in this system of economics into one state, enable them to establish themselves there in comparative comfort and ultimately, by colonizing a sufficient number of them, to take possession of the political machinery of that state, adopt a new constitution and through it establish the Co-operative Commonwealth.

"We who have enlisted in this enterprise believe that our own grand republic, with its system of interdependent yet sovereign states, offers the field for an experiment and an example which may enlighten the world. The example of Utah, although disapproved as to its purpose, presents an instance of a commonwealth developing under the influence of an idea.

"When the idea is pure and exalted, and at the same time furnishes hope to hungry and struggling millions, how much more likely is it to develop a masterpiece among states.

"The Co-operative Commonwealth is already organized.

"It even now numbers 3,000 votes, representing 15,000 people—men, women and children—in its membership.

"A fund of $100,000 has been accumulated and is now available to establish co-operative colonies and is rapidly increasing. No colonies, it is true, have been established, for the reason that we have not yet selected the state for that purpose. This selection is the special purpose of our meeting to-night.

"Let me express to you, my friends, the belief that we are now meeting in the most important convention which we have ever held, because our success depends undeniably upon the proper location of our Co-operative Commonwealth. Strong arguments can be produced in favor of the South and the West, and I have heard more favorable mention of Tennessee than of any of the states. I hope, gentlemen, that you will discuss this matter fully and deliberately as becomes the dignity and high purpose of men who, perhaps, are about to give to the world its most enduring and most beneficent commonwealth."

So the meeting was declared open for discussion. The gentlemen who participated were not partisans of any particular section or state and were evidently disposed to be deliberate and cautious in their selection. Most of them presented arguments in favor of Tennessee. Some were in favor of the state of Washington. As I listened to the discussion I was conscious of a deep feeling of interest developing within me. It seemed to me that intuitively I comprehended the motives and purposes of these men and that I had a stronger grasp upon the details of their design than they. A great inspiration seized upon me which seemed to swing my mind over every detail and to light up every feature of this subject. When all who intended appeared to have spoken, the chairman suggested that Mr. Braden might, perhaps, present some views which would be worthy of consideration. I could not forbear compliance and spoke as follows:

"Gentlemen—I feel a deep and profound sympathy for the objects of this meeting. When I say this I do not want to be understood as expressing favor for any plan whereby the thoughtful, conservative statesmanship of modern society is to be set aside, and experimental statesmanship is to be substituted for it. I am convinced that the social system which Christendom accepts to-day is the best which humanity has ever employed, and that it would be the worst of crimes to destroy it without furnishing some practical model for a new and better one.

"The United States presents a plan which is sufficiently elastic, an area sufficiently extensive, and opportunities sufficiently varied and abundant, to make it proper that one state should be devoted to the development of the co-operative system. I, for one, am fully convinced that a state should be selected in which the obstacles to your efforts will be but few and slight. For instance, you ought not to concentrate your efforts on Tennessee if there is another area, less populous, less prejudiced and less attached to the present system.

"The vote of Tennesee is 321,190. Its population approaches 2,000,000. You must, in order to gain control of Tennessee, increase its population by nearly 2,000,000 co-operators casting a vote of nearly 300,000. This assumes that a portion of the present population is not opposed to the Co-operative Commonwealth. It is plain to me that it will take you a generation to accomplish your purpose.

"The same objections apply in a less degree to Washington. The population of that state is 450,000 and its vote 93,435. To direct our colonies to a territory not yet admitted into the Union, like Arizona, New Mexico and Oklahoma, would subject them to repressive congressional legislation from which in a state they would be free. As for Wyoming, with a population of 60,000 and a vote of 21,000, it does not present a field for our operations as suitable as some others.

"For my part I am greatly prepossessed in favor of Idaho. It has an area of about 86,000 square miles, a population of about 90,000 and a vote of about 30,000. Its vote is now increased by, probably, 15,000 on account of the extension of the right of suffrage of women. This will be an advantage to your colonists, because the proportion of married men among you will be greater than that of the shifting population of the mining camps. It is evident that you will control the state as soon as you have 50,000 men and women there. Already the Co-operative Commonwealth numbers 3,000 men and this means 6,000 votes. But I make no doubt that 100,000 men, to say nothing of their wives, are ready to go to Idaho with your colonies if you choose that location.

"But you ask, what manner of place is Idaho? I reply, that in my journeyings throughout my beloved country I have found its superior nowhere in what goes to produce a great commonwealth. Its name signifies 'Light on the Mountains.' It has valleys of great breadth and fertility, mountains covered with extensive forests, lakes of enchanting beauty, navigable rivers, swift streams, unlimited water power, inexhaustible mineral resources.

"It has 12,000,000 acres of land which can be reclaimed by irrigation and made lavishly productive, and there is plenty of water available for the purpose. It has seven million acres of forest lands. You, perhaps, have no very great acquaintance with Idaho. This, in my opinion, should induce you to select a committee to visit the state incognito to examine and report on its resources. You will find that it is capable of supporting a population of 10,000,-

000 people. These can engage in manufacture, farming, grazing, fruit culture, mining, wool growing and all the pursuits followed by the people of Pennsylvania or New England. The climate is not so warm as that of Tennessee, but in my judgment that is an advantage. It is much warmer than in any northern state east of the Rockies and north of the Ohio river. It is dry and healthful.

"Gentlemen, I shall not enter into a further description of Idaho, but beg you to make an investigation. Remember that in states whose opportunities are famous those opportunities have been occupied. If you can find a state which is but little known you will find its opportunities open for you to take possession of and control. Idaho is such a state."

My remarks produced a deep impression. I was followed by several gentlemen who heartily approved the suggestion to appoint a committee of investigation and to send the committee to Idaho, to report after a month's absence. A motion to that effect was carried providing that the chairman and two others, to be appointed by him, should constitute that committee. The chairman did me the honor to appoint me, and also appointed Henry B. Henderson, a gentleman of great wealth, a reformer of thirty years' standing, and one of the truest and best men who ever graced the planet with an unselfish life. The assembly then adjourned to meet again a month after, when the committee was to make its report.

CHAPTER IV.

THE COMMISSION REPORTS AND IDAHO IS SELECTED — COLONY NUMBER ONE PREPARES TO ENTER THE LAND OF ITS CHOICE—THE JOURNEY TO HUNTINGTON, OREGON, AND INCIDENTS AT THAT PLACE—ON TO DEER VALLEY.

The commission to investigate the resources of Idaho performed their labors conscientiously and after an absence of about a month made such a report as determined our people to choose Idaho for the home of the society. This important detail being settled, it was decided to send Colony Number One into the field as speedily as possible. The commission had recommended a valley through which ran a small stream into Snake river as a suitable location. It was a beautiful valley, about twenty-five miles in length and from a quarter of one to five miles wide. The stream flowing from the high mountains near its source had never been known to fail, and poured its torrents with ceaseless power into the flood at its mouth.

The mountain rose only a short distance from its banks for ten miles along its course, but when it emerged from the foot hills the broad and fertile acres spread away on both sides until they reached the top of rich divides. In the mountains along its border grew great forests of yellow pine and gold and silver abounded. Gold had also been mined in placers all along the valley, and was still found in greater or less quantity. The soil was as rich as that of the Nile, and everywhere in the wild state the grasses grew luxuriant and nutritious.

The climate, we learned, was all that could be desired. Surrounded by high mountains and plateaus and nestling in the depths of an immense depression, extreme climatic changes were unknown. The winters were as mild as those of Southern Ohio and the Chinook winds from the warm

Pacific currents breathed over this region, now and then, the balmy sympathy of southern climes.

Colony Number One was fully organized with John Thompson as President, Henderson as Treasurer and myself as Secretary. The number of our members was then three hundred. We were not limited by any law or rule as to our membership, but had decided to accept no more applications until we were fully established in our western home. It was arranged that fifty men should go to the selected location and make the necessary preparations for the colony. Thompson, Henderson and myself were included. The other forty-seven were made up of mechanics, farmers and lumbermen.

There were six farmers, six lumber and sawmill men, six carpenters, three masons, three stonecutters, three expert sheep men, three expert cattle men, three merchants, one physician, one blacksmith, one horseshoer, and eleven who, although men of intelligence and able to adapt themselves to all kinds of work, were not trained to any special calling. These fifty paid into the colony treasury one hundred dollars each; fifty others, who were expected to follow us in three months, paid in twenty-five dollars; fifty more paid fifteen dollars; fifty others paid ten dollars, and the remainder five. All these were to continue payments at the same rate monthly until the entrance fee of one hundred dollars was paid, when the member would become entitled to enter the colony as an active colonist. We found ourselves possessed, then, on the day of our departure, of eight thousand five hundred dollars, paid in by members, and the Brotherhood throughout the United States loaned us ten thousand dollars from its accumulated fund, to be repaid in three years.

Our faith and credit, as honest men, were the only security the Brotherhood required. Each man paid his own fare and traveling expenses until we reached Huntington, in Eastern Oregon. From that point until we arrived at our destination all expenses were to be borne in common and defrayed from the common fund.

It was agreed that until the colony was entirely established, and its business had reached a tolerably settled condition, John Thompson should have larger powers than the presidential office conferred upon him. This was done because it was thought the exigencies and uncertainties of the situation demanded his varied experience and the exercise of his quick judgment and large executive force. We regarded him as a sort of military chief, although we were as little like a military band as it would be possible to conceive. He naturally assumed the leadership and we naturally submitted to it. The better to direct our movements he divided us into squads of six, putting the carpenters into a squad numbered one, and directing them to choose a foreman; the masons and stonecutters together numbered two; the sheep and cattle men numbered three; the lumber and sawmill men numbered four; the merchants, blacksmith, horseshoer and one commoner numbered five; the farmers numbered six; six commoners numbered seven; Henderson, myself and four commoners, all of the latter being educated men, one an ex-editor, one an ex-clergyman and one an assayer and chemist and another a surveyor and ex-real estate man, numbered eight. The physician was not included in any squad but was, as we facetiously declared, to constitute a squad by himself.

May 1st, 1897, we took our departure from Chicago for our future home, and proceeding over the Union Pacific arrived at Huntington in due time. Disembarking here, we went into camp on the outskirts of the little town and commenced the purchase of our necessary outfit.

Before leaving Chicago we had purchased and caused to be shipped to us a stock of groceries, hardware, a limited quantity of dry goods, drugs, paints, a number of ploughs, harrows and farm and mining tools and tools for our mechanics, a portable sawmill and eight farm wagons at a cost of nine thousand dollars in all. These were all at Huntington when we arrived. But we were without live stock, horses or seed. Thompson, who had been conceded the title of captain, assigned to each squad its duty.

. . . .

Number One received orders to take charge of one wagon and load the same with such tools as carpenters required, and if any room was left over to report to him. Number Two assumed charge of a second wagon with similar instructions. Number Three did the same with the third wagon, but was also directed to purchase, in the surrounding country, ten milch cows, a herd of one hundred and fifty cattle and one thousand sheep. Number Four was instructed to take one wagon and in addition to provide for the transportation of the portable sawmill. Numbers Five, Six, Seven and Eight were each assigned to a wagon, and Thompson, with the aid of two members of Number Six, who were excellent horsemen, undertook the purchase of the horses.

We sojourned in the neighborhood of Huntington a week. At the end of that time our company was prepared to move. We had purchased a quantity of seed for two hundred dollars, sixteen draft horses at a cost of eight hundred dollars, and forty-two saddle horses at a cost of eight hundred and forty dollars. We had acquired our milch cows for two hundred dollars, one hundred and fifty cattle for two thousand dollars and a flock of sheep numbering one thousand for fifteen hundred dollars, and there remained four thousand dollars in our treasury.

The road from Huntington was quite familiar to "The Captain" and myself. Both of us, but at different periods, had spent considerable time in the vicinity of Huntington and had explored along Snake river and its tributaries for gold. We were able, therefore, to point out a suitable road and as we proceeded upon our journey we encountered no obstacles except when we found it necessary to cross Snake river.

This obstacle only served to delay us a short time, there being at that point a ferry which we employed to take us across. Once in Idaho our people seemed to acquire new life. Everything was full of interest. We made no effort to march in any regular system except that the squad wagons followed each other in numerical order, the bull train, which had been **hired to transport** the portable **sawmill, following** somewhat slowly **far in** the rear. The men in charge of the machinery were residents of Huntington **and** well acquainted with the road to our destination, which was then known as Deer Valley.

As we moved along we found the country settled, **but** somewhat sparsely. Here **and there** a rancher came out to salute us and, learning **of our intention to** settle in Idaho, bade us a hearty welcome. Sometimes we fell in with cowboys in charge of herds of cattle, and passed through several camps of miners who worked the placers along Snake river. Several of these latter **were** composed of Chinese and their workings were referred to by the white miners **in other camps** as "Chinese Diggings." We observed that everywhere the soil was rich but lacking in moisture except **where** irrigation was employed. The grasses, although the season was early, were luxuriant and the cattle, which had wintered without shelter, were **in** remarkably good condition.

Several of the large ranches were among the most beautiful I had ever seen. One of these, comprising about five **hundred acres, was located where** a swift stream, called Conner creek, flowed into Snake river. This stream had been tapped at a **high** elevation and **the waters diverted, by means of** a flume, to the rich **alluvial lands below.** There a system of small ditches distributed the waters among orchards of peaches, apples, pears, plums, nectarines and apricots and among vineyards of grapes and beds of strawberries. The rancher who had charge of this wonderful little domain, **a** portly old man, full of information, **affable** and communicative, assured me that he had **traveled the** world over but had never beheld a fairer **spot** than this. "But," said he, "Idaho is filled with **such places."**

I asked him about the markets **and he candidly** informed **me** that he had been unable to **garner and ship** his fruits, lacking funds for that **purpose, but that he had** sold his vegetables at a good profit in the neighboring mining camps. He also showed us a large quantity of dried fruit which his son had cut and prepared and which there was a market for in the same camps.

"But," he said, "I have not found the South to be as profitable for farming as this locality, because if their market is more extensive it is also far cheaper. At the outset the advantage is with us. Our grain, hay, hogs and vegetables are all readily disposed of and command a good price among the gold mines."

Such incidents, and the sublime scenery which everywhere presented itself to our delighted vision, varied the monotony of our journey so that the three days spent on the way after crossing Snake river seemed to pass like a dream. We arrived at Deer Valley without any accident of a serious nature, full of hope, in the best of health and eager to begin the work of laying, as it were, the cornerstone of the Co-operative Commonwealth.

CHAPTER V.

DEER VALLEY—THE FOUNDING AND NAMING OF CO-OPOLIS—THOMPSON'S AND EDMUNDS' VIEWS.

It was about noon on the 20th day of May, 1897, that our company entered Deer Valley. We found a very good road leading up into the mountains along the south bank of the stream and followed that without difficulty. The captain, taking six of our horsemen, including myself, went ahead of the rest of the company, who followed after more slowly with the wagons and live stock. The sawmill machinery was nearly a day's journey behind them.

The captain's purpose was to select a suitable site for a camp which would in all probability be more permanent than we had yet made. He was quite familiar with Deer Valley, as I have already stated, and had in mind a location which on other occasions he had marked as an excellent place in which to build a city. In a short time we arrived at this place and commenced an examination of the surroundings. We all readily agreed that the captain's judgment was good and, after viewing the land from many points, unanimously decided to recommend it to our company as a proper place to establish our camp.

We were about four miles from Snake river. The valley at this point was somewhat over five miles wide, walled in by table lands on either side. These table lands were high elevations with level summits covering many square miles of fertile but dry lands. They sloped from the summits through a succession of three shelves, each quite level, down toward the valley, and thence the valley inclined gently toward the river bed. The stream itself flowed at the bottom of a deep gully and its banks were prettily fringed with box elder trees. The table lands, their sloping sides, the shelves and the broad area of the valley down to the fringe of box elder trees, presented at this season of the year a beautiful sight.

All was dressed in the verdure of the rich grasses which make the highlands and lowlands of Idaho famous as the grazing grounds of those great herds of cattle which abundantly assist in feeding the world. There were a few trees in places on the slopes of the highlands, and a hillock which was proposed as the location of our camp, contained quite a grove. But except for these, and the fringe of box elders along the river bank, the entire area was quite open. The stream at this time came tumbling down the valley at a furious rate, the incline being quite pronounced. Looking up the valley we saw the giant mountains on whose majestic tops the snow remained unmelted, and whose lower sides were black with the foliage of the forest of yellow pine.

We found here a rancher who claimed to be the owner of some three hundred and twenty acres of land which he had attempted to reclaim by means of a rather crude irrigating ditch which conducted the water of the stream from a point above to a portion of his ground. He claimed also to have washed some gold from the sand taken from the bed of the creek. The man had lived in the valley for ten years, but was evidently neither a man of enterprise nor much intelligence. He had once possessed a considerable herd, but had lost it at the gaming table in some of the camps, and was poor and anxious to get away into the "diggings," up in the mountains. He was able to give some information of value to us, and offered to sell us the ranch and about a hundred acres of land which he held under the placer mining laws of the United States, for two dollars an acre.

We were occupied in making these observations when, about two hours after our arrival, the wagons and their escort reached a point on the road near the house (it was scarcely more than a hut) of the old rancher. The captain and myself immediately rode over and directions were

THE CO-OPOLITAN. 27

given to proceed to the hillock, where the grove of young trees already mentioned offered an inviting shelter, and go into camp. Accordingly the entire company went thither, the teams were unharnessed, the horses were picketed, some tents were pitched and the men were soon to be seen engaged in conversation in little groups, some standing on elevations which offered a commanding view, others moving to various parts of the valley, and others still, lying down and making observations while they rested. The farmers were particularly industrious, looking over old Hacket's ranch.

As the afternoon of this memorable first day wore to its close the men all returned to camp, where those to whom the duty of preparing meals had been assigned had prepared a feast somewhat more elaborate than usual, and one of them reminded us that this was the first feast on the site of our new town and that the anniversary of this day would hereafter be a feast day for years to come. The prophecy was hailed with approval and the evening was given up to feasting and speaking, just as has been customary on this anniversary ever since.

After the meal was finished we gathered together under one of the largest trees in the grove and called upon those who were known to be speakers to address us. Among others the company called on me and I proposed that, as we were to have a city, whether it be established on the spot or in some other place, and as our city must have a name, that we proceed to give it a name forthwith. To this one of the company, Albert Ortz, a German, objected, for the reason that our sheep and cattle men, as well as four of our commoners, being in charge of the herds which had not yet arrived, ought to be allowed to take part. To this I replied that our action would not be binding, if we selected a name, and we could regard the selection now as merely informal. This was satisfactory and Ortz withdrew his objection. I then called for names to be voted on. Three only were submitted. Alpha, because it was the first of its kind; Co-opolis, the city of co-operators, and Omega, which Dr. Pinder proposed, because, he said rather facetiously, our co-operative city was about the last hope which labor had left for justice in this world. The vote was then taken and resulted in a large majority for Co-opolis. It is as well to say here that afterward our absent members voted unanimously to approve this name, and the city was so christened.

While this was going on the captain had said nothing and, I observed, did not even vote. He had been sitting somewhat apart from the rest of the company with a half-pleased but yet serious look upon his face. I had come to understand him very well, and knew that he felt grave apprehensions for the success of this movement, and now I made no doubt that he was feeling the responsibility which rested upon each member of the colony.

"Brothers," said I, "I notice that our captain is serious when he should be gay. I, for one, vote that the captain give an account of himself."

Everybody called for the captain.

"My brothers," said he, in response, "I regret that you have called upon me to speak, because the thoughts which press for expression are not altogether in harmony with the gayety of our present festivities. I am sure that none rejoices more than I do for the safe arrival of our party in this beautiful valley. But my mind is not with to-day nor yesterday, but dwells with the future. The project which has brought us here is, in the light of all history, an exceedingly ambitious one. Failure, it is true, cannot result injuriously, but success will be a beacon light of hope to those many millions of men and women who are denied access to nature's countless bounties.

"You, my brothers, have wives and children who will follow you ere long into this fair country. For you, as individuals, the world is opening out its avenues of comfort, but upon each of us here rests a responsibility such as few men have ever assumed. We are here not merely to benefit ourselves, but to benefit, by the force of example, the waiting and watching world.

"Co-operative enterprises have been successful in many commercial and mechanical pursuits. As a rule such enterprises have failed so far as land and its cultivation are concerned. But there is no apparent reason why they should be less successful than are the enterprises of commerce and manufacture. Our purpose is to combine all laborious or productive occupations. Behold, my brothers, this beautiful valley! God has secreted in almost every inch of its soil the gift of productivity. Yonder the mountains tower above us. God has made the forest to yield fuel and lumber for our use. High up on the white-capped summits and deep down in the cool cisterns of nature are the sources of these waters which flow in the rushing torrent, and which we may direct thither to moisten this soil. On the table lands which rise north and south of us our herds and flocks shall graze.

"You can see, my brothers, that if we fail in our enterprise the fault will be in us and not in nature. The duty which lies before us is to work in harmony. We must encourage competition in all lines of mental, physical and spiritual progress. But we must rid ourselves of competition in the simple acquisition of property. We must encourage individualism in all that makes men practical, self-reliant and manly. We must destroy it in all that makes men grasping and unsympathetic.

"My brothers, the great world beyond deems that man greatest who acquires the greatest fortune or wields the greatest power, but I say to you that man is greatest who induces the greatest number of men and women to do right. Such is the manhood we must honor, and upon the brow of such we shall place the laurel wreath of victory. If we work to such a purpose we shall succeed.

"My brothers, the most difficult part of our project lies in our foundation work. We will meet obstacles. Some of our number may, perhaps, be of opinion that the first year or two of our struggle here should be free from difficulty because our ideal is high. If so it were better that those immediately return to their eastern homes, because there is nothing for us, the pioneers of the Co-operative Commonwealth, but arduous labor. Your wives and children look forward to a time when they may come hither to homes which you have established where the old system which has forced you into this unsettled country cannot affect them. What will you do? Will you subjugate self, defer to one another's opinions, and work always together, and so make your enterprise succeed? I believe you will.

"My brothers, this work is in your hands. I have been your leader thus far, but I now surrender the leadership and insist that the will of the majority be your guide hereafter."

When Thompson ceased to speak some seconds elapsed before any one ventured to break silence. His words were fully appreciated and it was evident that all comprehended the magnitude of the task whic hwas before them. Mr. Edmunds, ex-clergyman, voiced the general sentiment of all.

"You are not alone, Brother Thompson," said he, "in your apprehensions. Most of us entertain the same doubts as to the future which you have expressed. But it is better it should be so than that we should, in such an enterprise, be carried away by enthusiasm. When soldiers approach the dangers of war, where death and glory mingle, their captain seeks to inspire them with a courage which dares but does not reason. No need of that with us. The task we have to accomplish is, in truth, devoid of danger. It is the easiest ever proposed to the intelligence of man. All that we need lies where God placed it centuries ago, and is ours, if only we will take it. If we make this task hard, it is because we will not reason. If dangers arise, they will not arise from the mountain, stream or valley, nor yet from yonder table lands nor grassy slopes. They will arise from ourselves. This we must study to avoid. This is our work. One thing, my brothers, we must do from the outset. Let our community be self-dependent. Let us call upon the outside world to help us as little as possible. Let us build our own homes, burn our own lime, manufacture our own furniture and crockery. Let us make it a rule that whatever we can make ourselves, no matter how much labor it costs us, that we will make. If we do this and work together success is certain."

The clergyman spoke for nearly half an hour and finished amid great enthusiasm, for his speech was able and brilliant and calculated to produce confidence in our enterprise.

This ended the memorable first day.

CHAPTER VI.

THE GENERAL SYSTEM—PROGRESS THE FIRST YEAR—
LAND TITLES—LABOR ORDERS.

The city of Co-opolis was established, after the surrounding region was duly explored, upon the site of our first camp in Deer Valley. The Hacket ranch and water rights were acquired by our company at a small expense, the farmers went to work upon it immediately and in a comparatively short time we had many acres of land broken and planted. We sowed very little wheat the first year, but made a specialty of corn, calculating that we could feed it to our cattle and hogs, and believing that we could realize more from our live stock than from the raising and sale of wheat. We also planted vegetables of all kinds in quantities which we believed would not only suffice for our company for the following winter, but would enable us to dispose of a surplus in the mining camps in the mountains.

The ex-surveyor, meanwhile, proceeded to lay out a town. This was a very simple task, as our plan was to construct a public hall and office building in the center of a large square, surround the latter by a wide street, and erect our store, hotel and residences on this street. If the city grew it was considered that we had ample space at our command. Meanwhile the sawmill had arrived and had been conveyed to a place on the banks of the stream and placed in charge of the sawmill men. One of these having great experience in the forests of Wisconsin, took a number of picked commoners and went to the headwaters of the stream in the mountains and was soon able to send a large quantity of pine logs down the current, where they were caught and sawed into lumber of various dimensions. In three weeks after we started our camp our carpenters had built a temporary frame store building, a rather crude hotel and had supplied these with furniture which was rather crude and unfinished but sufficient for our purposes. It was not considered prudent to erect any permanent structures until our lumber should become better seasoned, but carpenters, masons and stonecutters proceeded to excavate for the fifty cottages which we designed to construct for our members and their families. In the latter part of June, such was our industry, we had a very respectable appearing village, with carpenter and blacksmith shops and general store. The last was the feature of the village, containing a stock of hardware, dry goods and groceries and a stock of drugs of various kinds. The hotel furnished board and lodging to all our company.

Shortly after our arrival at Co-opolis, at a series of meetings held for that purpose, we had formed our permanent organization, taken as our name "The Co-opolitan Association" and adopted a constitution and by-laws to regulate our colony.

The constitution dealt only with the system of government and invested the lawmaking body, which it created, with unlimited powers as to all other matters.

The President was to hold office for seven years and was ineligible to re-election.

The Vice-President was elected for the same period.

The first President and Vice-President were elected by all active members, and any member was eligible, but after seven years these officers must be elected from among heads of departments only.

Heads of departments were to be denominated chiefs and were to be chosen by popular vote from among foremen and the latter by the Legislative Council.

The lawmaking power was to consist of the heads of departments and President and Vice-President, the former presiding at all legislative meetings and the latter, by virtue of his office, being a member of the Legislative Council with the right to speak and vote on all propositions.

Whenever twenty per cent of the men and women of the Association should petition the Legislative Council to declare any office vacant it was bound to submit the question as to whether such vacancy should be so declared to popular vote, and if a majority decided in the affirmative then the Council must declare it. The incumbent whose office or position was thus vacated was not eligible again for the remainder of his unexpired term and the full term following.

Officers found guilty by the Council of misfeasance or malfeasance in office were also subject to impeachment by the Council, who were required to pass on the particular charges submitted to them.

The legislative and judicial functions were both conferred upon the Legislative Council, and this body could initiate and complete legislation, but on petition of twenty per cent of all voters proposing a new law the Legislative Council was required to submit such law to popular vote and the decision of a majority of such voters operated as either an enactment or repeal. This action was effectual to permanently dispose of such law for five years. The constitution was also subject to revision, correction, amendment or repeal by the same method.

The constitution further provided that every person under twenty years of age should be in charge of the department of education, that no man or woman should in any event be required to work more than twenty-five years, but that after having contributed twenty-five years' labor should become entitled to his full share of the profits distributed annually among members.

This constitution did not limit the right of the people to shorten the term of service if they so desired. It was deemed expedient to provide for two classes of industrials, wage workers and members. The former were such as were employed and paid reasonable wages. These were rarely employed except in cases of emergency. The latter were such as had paid an entrance fee and had been accepted as equal partners in the enterprise. The wage workers were such as enlisted in the Industrial Army for pay and they could not participate in the affairs of the society **or** settlement. But **any one of these** who was in good health and of **sound mind could** become a member on payment **of the fee required and on** enlisting in the Industrial Army subject to the laws of the society.

No person was admitted who was over fifty-five years **of** age except such person was able to contribute to the Association's accumulated wealth **an amount** of property equal to the full annual dividend **of the average** member at the time of his application, multiplied by the number of years' service required by members. In later years, as is well known, the constitution does not admit an applicant who is over forty except on the same terms.

The constitution was by no means a perfect one at the outset, but it was sufficiently elastic and stable in its provisions to admit of such amendments, without danger to its substantial features, as might, from time to time, be suggested by experience.

The most conservative force in society has been found to be, not the wise nor the foolish, but the majority which are neither the one or the other. These are not generally fa**vorable** to experimental legislation, and long before the establishment of the Co-operative Commonwealth Switzerland proved, by the operation of the Initiative and Referendum provisions of their constitution, that the people were disposed to accept changes in their social system with a caution that made progress slow, but retrogression impossible.

The first year of the Co-operative Commonwealth was a very successful one. We had May 1st, 1898, over one thousand persons, including men, women and children, in our city of Co-opolis, two hundred and fifty substantial cottages, an excellent public hall, a good hotel, a large and sightly three-story building containing our department store, postoffice and offices for our President, Vice-President and heads of departments; an excellent schoolhouse with graded school and a corps of eight teachers, consisting of our ex-clergyman, who became first principal, and teachers who were selected from among the wives of members.

All the furniture used in our homes and buildings at this time was manufactured of such lumber as we had and was somewhat crude, but sufficient in all respects. In our department store were sold vegetables produced by us, consisting of potatoes, onions, beets, parsnips and all of the hardy variety grown on the old time "breaking" on Hacket's ranch. We had home-made preserves and a quantity of dried fruit. The meat department was well supplied from our own herds of cattle or from the surrounding country, and from our flocks of sheep, which had largely increased, partly through natural causes and partly because much of the money received for membership fees had been invested in that direction.

Shortly after we had definitely settled upon a site for Co-opolis we proceeded to acquire land. This whole valley was what in the United States land office was denominated "desert land," not because it was barren but because it was unproductive unless reclaimed by irrigation. Under the law it was permitted that each man enter three hundred and twenty acres upon declaring his intention to reclaim the same, and we had in this manner entered, up to June 1st, some sixteen thousand acres.

We had also, for the purpose of complying with the law and completing our titles, proceeded to a point about ten miles up the stream, and had there constructed a dam, collecting the waters of the stream by that means, and were engaged, whenever the weather permitted, in excavating ditches, or building flumes so as to conduct a large quantity of water nearly the whole length of the valley, but high up on the slopes of the "tables" on the south. The work was by no means finished, but it was easily estimated that when our plant was completed over eighty thousand acres of land would be available for agricultural purposes. That was on one side of the river. Our plans also included the irrigation of the north side of the river in the same manner. The law was such that, being the owners of Hacket's water right, and having tapped the stream at a time that no other settlers could be disturbed or interfered with, we were entitled to the exclusive control of the stream. We found that the law reqiured us to file our claims to this water right for record in the office of the Register of Deeds for the county, and did so accordingly. It was not difficult for any one of our number to see that we were in a position to shut out all settlers in this valley who were not members. The water right was taken in the names of Thompson, myself, Henderson, Ortz and three others, who constituted our first Legislative Council, as trustees for the Association. If any member who entered the land thought to segregate his tract ultimately from the great body of land he had only to consider that it was entirely worthless without irrigation, and that this was exclusively controlled by the Association.

The Industrial Army at this time numbered five hundred, one hundred and fifty being women and three·hundred and fifty men. The women were engaged largely in the Domestic department, but a number were employed in the departments of Commerce and Education. One of the merchants had charge of the department store, but most of the clerical help was selected from among the women. The bookkeepers were, at that time, all women. The chief of the Domestic department was a woman and as such participated in all our legislative councils. The entire army was divided into companies of twenty, and at the head of each company was a foreman. Each company was again divided into two squads of ten and each squad had a second or assistant foreman. In forming companies or squads our chiefs endeavored to have the members composed, as nearly as possible, of men having the same or kindred trades. We now had three physicians, one of whom was regarded as an especially skillful surgeon. We also had an incipient brass band which assisted largely in rendering the hours of recreation pleasant.

At this time we had a rapidly increasing trade at our store and were supplying many of the camps with such goods as they needed. Two of our own wagons were constantly employed in conveying groceries, hardware and other ware to our customers in the mountains, and it was not an uncommon thing for five or six wagons to come down in the course of a day for goods. The enterprise was successful and the prices which we obtained for what we sold were very profitable. We were obliged, however, to constantly replenish our stock of groceries, dry goods, hardware and drugs from the east. We also sold large quantities of beef in the mountains and, not caring to draw too heavily on our own herds for this demand, we kept a number of men constantly employed hunting and purchasing animals suitable for the purpose. We also devoted a building to the sick and our hospital was already quite famous throughout the entire region. Men in the camps who were injured or who had become sick preferred to endure the journey to Co-opolis to avail themselves of our physicians and nurses rather than risk the rough and sometimes reckless treatment to which they were elsewhere exposed. Our hotel, store and hospital were sources of profit which aided us largely the first and second years of our career.

One of the most difficult problems which we had to solve the first year was that of providing a medium of exchange for the use of our own members and also such persons as we might employ. We recognized that, although the money of society was at variance and inconsistent with all our plans, until we had fully established the Co-operative Commonwealth and acquired the state and all it contained, it would be impossible to establish a labor-check system. We decided that money was to be treated as a mere commodity and purchased as such, just as potatoes, wheat or beef were purchased. In dealing with the world outside of our society we must have money until we should become independent of it. It was on that theory that we endeavored to keep our fund of United States currency increasing.

How to deal among ourselves was the question. We were satisfied that members should, as nearly as possible, receive equal shares of what was produced in our colony, provided they were industrious and worked honestly, but we deemed that in the formative period of the commonwealth it was inexpedient to adopt the check system of Bellamy's social plan exclusively. We did, however, decide that checks should be given to those who desired them, but that, owing to the fact that many of our workers were to be, at the outset, mere hired men, it would be better to issue orders for each one's share as measured by dollars. The laws of the United States practically denied us the right to issue money or circulating notes, and our purpose was to build our state in entire harmony with the constitution. We proposed to avoid a conflict with the Federal government.

It was therefore decided that each member should receive wages, to be established upon the basis of a distribution of sixty per cent of all the society produced, equally divided among all persons above the age of twenty-one, whether male or female.

The forty per cent undistributed was to be used to purchase money for the use of the department store; in other words, sold for cash. These wages were to be paid in orders on the treasurer, signed by the president. They were required to read as follows: "To the Treasurer of the Co-opolitan Association: Deliver to John Jenkins, Foreman of Company Number One of the Industrial Army, one (or any denomination) dollar's worth of any product, convenience, privilege or license at your disposal. Signed, John Thompson, President."

These orders were to be delivered to the foreman only and it was the foreman's duty to endorse or stamp his name on the back so that, when once so endorsed or stamped, they became current as a medium of exchange, but not as a measure of value. The foreman's duty was to pay his men with these orders and he was held to the strictest account for the disposition made of each order. Whenever an order was received in any department it was stamped canceled and never again issued. Most of our members for the first three years preferred the check. As time passed, however, the credit labor check became more and more popular and in time crowded out the circulating orders entirely.

CHAPTER VII.

CO-OPOLIS A CONVENTION CITY—A MENACE TO LIBERTY.

It was a bright day in the latter part of June, 1902, that the first state convention of the Co-operative Commonwealth met in our city of Co-opolis to place in nomination a full state ticket for the state of Idaho. It was considered that the co-operators were strong enough to take possession of the political machinery of the state. The National Brotherhood, using Co-opolis as a basis for its operations in the state, had directed many colonies to Co-opolis and we had taken charge of them as they came, absorbed most of them in our own Industrial Army, and others we had assisted to establish themselves in some fertile valley in the state where they could put their own peculiar ideas and methods of co-operation into practice.

We now had fifty thousand male and female voters, upon whose solid support we could count to carry out our designs. Most of this population was settled through the southern, central and western part of the state, and there were at least forty cities and villages entirely devoted to our cause. Co-opolis contained a population of fifteen thousand souls—men, women and children. Its Industrial Army was 7,000 strong, and its members, working not more than seven hours a day, accomplished the most remarkable results.

Co-opolis itself, while not comparable with the present great city, was at that time the fairest city on the face of the earth. I say this not because it could or did boast of massive structures, splendid palaces or costly monuments, for these were absent, but because there was not a mean or dilapidated building in it and there was not a pauper among all its people. Millionaires were not numerous, but there were several rich men, all of whom, except Thompson, whose father had died leaving him a vast estate, and Henderson, who had always been accounted wealthy, were visitors, or resided in the city to have the advantage of its hotel and climate. These latter, be it said in passing, boarded at the Co-opolitan hotel or rented cottages of the Association. There were some excellent buildings, among which were numbered the great store of the Department of Commerce, which had now grown to vast proportions. The building was four stories high and occupied nearly an ordinary city block. The larger part of the goods exposed for sale were produced in Co-opolis.

In the next block to this structure, on the site of the present Co-opolitan Hall, was one which more modern Co-opolis has placed there, but which had a seating capacity of 10,000, and was the largest and best equipped in the state. With the grounds belonging to it the hall occupied an entire block. The next block contained a very sightly high school edifice and its grounds.

All the avenues in the city were so laid out that they consisted each of a park fifty feet wide with a driveway of equal width on each side and resembled in some respects the boulevards of Paris. The parks were well-kept lawns, surrounded by young trees and traversed by gravel walks. The driveways were all paved with asphalt, as were also the country roads extending in every direction for one mile beyond the city proper. All avenues and streets were lined with young, thrifty trees, planted by the Association.

All buildings were required to be at least fifty feet apart, and the spaces between were arranged according to the taste of the occupants of the houses. There were no fences in the city. Commonwealth Avenue contained the several department offices and storage buildings. There were three electric railroads, which were owned in common by all the cities, co-operative towns and communities of the state which at this time centered in Co-opolis. The congest was one hundred and fifty miles and extended to Boise, the Capital of the state.

The transcontinent **roads** also entered the city. But **the** application of electricity **to** nearly all locomotion had enabled the city to preserve its streets from being marred and rendered unsightly and dangerous by **street** railroads. The **electric** motorcycles, bicycles **and** tricycles, operated by storage batteries, which plied rapidly along the smooth and clean asphalt streets, were the pleasing harbingers of that system **by which we are now** enabled to travel **on** similar roads **throughout the length and breadth of** fair and favored Idaho.

The scene presented by the streets of Co-opolis, on this convention **day**, was inspiring. Everywhere the American **flag was** displayed, and sentiments of patriotism filled the **air. It** was **a** gala day. Not only had the delegates to the **convention** congregated in the city, but friends and enemies seemed to have thought the event an extremely important one **and** came from all parts of the state, as well as from Western Oregon. **At nine o'clock in** the morning groups **of people—men** and women—wandered through the streets, **viewing the** city, and **all** the public vehicles, motorcycles, **bicycles,** tricycles and carriages, were employed in the **same service.** For the accommodation and refreshment of **visitors the** Commerce department had caused little refreshment fountains to be stationed in different parts of the **city,** along the avenues, **and in the** parks, containing cool **and pleasant drinks,** and lunch counters, in charge of mem**bers** of that department, were also located in places. These **supplied** the **public** needs at nominal prices. There were **also** pavilions **in the** parks every six blocks where tired wanderers **could rest** themselves.

As **the chief of** the Messenger and Publishing departments I had charge of the telephones, telegraphs and public press of the Association. The Daily Co-opolitan was the only newspaper which this department published at that time, but the department was required by our law to publish whatever any member or association of members was willing to pay for at reasonable rates. The Co-opolitan, however, had **no mission** but the publication of news, pub-

THE CO-OPOLITAN. 43

lic opinions as represented by articles appearing in other papers, and such articles as might be contributed, if the contributors signed them. Anonymous editorials or articles were prohibited and nothing appeared while the paper was under my charge except what my judgment or that of my staff approved. My position was one of great importance, because I was practically in control of public opinion. I hope I did not abuse my power and at this time am not conscious that I did so. The opportunity for such abuse has since been removed by the establishment of many other papers all printed and distributed by the Association, but controlled and edited by persons who advocate their own views.

Seated in the general office of my department that morning running over the columns of the Co-opolitan, I noticed an editorial copied from the Boston Transcript of recent date entitled "A Menace to Liberty." I immediately read it and found that it was a direct attack on the Co-opolitan Association. It classed the movement with the Mormon occupation of Utah; declared that it was hostile to a republican form of government; asserted that the men who had become most prominent in pushing it to the front were designing and ambitious persons who sought only their own aggrandizement and alleged that it had become so powerful in Idaho as to threaten to take control of the state and set up a government which the constitution of the nation forbade. It was particularly severe on John Thompson. "This man," it said, "is reported to be an illiterate but able man, possessed of great executive force, who has conceived the entire plan and has superintended with remarkable diligence and ability the details of its development. As President of the company he is the practical uncrowned king of Idaho. This scheme to embrace a state within the dominion of one company is the most daring and dangerous yet attempted by corporate greed. Should it succeed, grave constitutional questions will arise and congress will be called upon to deal with this new menace to liberty and good morals as it did with the Mormon question.

"There is this difference, however, that the monopolistic octopus now threatening Idaho is entrenched behind an unfortunate system which recognizes the independence of states and the obnoxious doctrine of state rights, while the Mormons, being in a territory which was directly within the jurisdiction of congress, were struck down by the sentiment of the entire Union made effective by national legislation. But as our people found means to rend the veil of this obnoxious doctrine, to strike down slavery in the South, so it will find a way to rend it again and strike down such institutions as this so-called Co-operative Commonwealth or Co-opolitan Association."

I threw the paper down upon the floor with an expression and feeling of indignation. I knew that our movement had attracted wide attention, but never before had I seen any indication of hostility. The newspaper press of the United States had generally treated the undertaking as an experiment which would teach a useful lesson if successful, but waived it aside as purely idealistic and not likely to succeed. Now one of the most conservative and reputable metropolitan dailies in the country, ignoring all its former expressions of approval, had deliberately reversed itself, suppressed facts, falsified the truth, and, on the eve of the success of the co-operative programme in Idaho, had begun a campaign for its destruction. So entirely consumed was I, for the moment, by my own passion that I did not notice the entrance of President Thompson and was somewhat startled when he saluted me.

"Brother Braden," said he, "you seem to be disturbed about something."

"Yes," I replied. "Look at that article from the Boston Transcript and see whether I, and we, have not cause to be troubled."

"I have seen it," calmly rejoined he. "But," he continued, "I am not surprised. Having read extensively and seen much I have learned that men are quite likely to view with complacency, and sometimes approval, the development of an idea, but the moment that idea becomes formidable they attack it. I expect, in fact, that we will win the coming election in this state, but when we call our constitutional convention I am by no means certain that we will get the majority of delegates."

"Indeed," said I, "I have never heard you talk so doubtfully before."

"I know it, Braden," replied Thompson. "The occasion has never before arisen. You will find, however, that the battle for the Co-operative Commonwealth has just begun. I have come over to see you now about the convention. Our friends are asking me to be the candidate for governor. I have not been inclined to accept, but I would be glad if you will give me your opinion as to whether I ought to do so."

"You must do so," I exclaimed. "I have not expected anything else. I know that you consider your position as President of the Co-operative Commonwealth an objection to your assuming other duties. It is not. You should retain both positions. Why, sir, I expect that when the new constitution is framed it will provide for a President whose term of office will be commensurate with the term of our President and that the officers of one will be the officers of the other. I expect that this dual character will continue to exist until every trace of property individualism has disappeared and that then, instead of the Co-operative Commonwealth being Idaho, Idaho will be the Co-operative Commonwealth."

It was evident that the view so expressed made an impression on Thompson. We talked it over for nearly an hour and when the time arrived for the convention to meet it was practically decided that, if the convention should so desire, Thompson would accept the nomination for governor.

CHAPTER VIII.

THE FIRST CO-OPERATIVE CONVENTION—THOMPSON NOMINATED FOR GOVERNOR.

The great hall was thronged with delegates and spectators. There was a feeling that this convention was to select the next governor and state officers and people who were not members, but resided in Idaho, were many of them disposed to be favorable. The railroads, owners of gold mines, some of the great cattle kings, real estate brokers, money loaners and saloons were against us, but the masses were friendly. We calculated that we had ten thousand more votes at our disposal than our opponents. It was estimated by the leaders of the People's party that more than half of the inhabitants of the state outside of the Association would support the ticket, but Thompson had several times assured me that while more than half were disposed to support us, most of them had not the mental strength to do so. Be that as it may the convention met, organized and went to work. No need to describe all that was done. Mr. Edmunds, chief of our Department of Education, made a speech nominating John Thompson for governor. He described the Co-opolitan Association, presented an historical sketch of its foundation and development, pictured Co-opolis as it was when our company reached Hacket's ranch, told the story of each year's work, and, in closing, showed how one master mind conceived and one master spirit directed every detail of that magnificent undertaking.

"You would hardly credit, if you were acquainted with the facts, the history of Co-opolis as I have presented it," said he as he proceeded. "From the smallest beginnings we have progressed to that magnificent estate which lies before you. The world may behold if it will, and accept the model if it choose. In five years all this has been effected.

In the first year we had only the bare land, the running water, a few cattle and sheep. In the second year we had five thousand cultivated acres, ten thousand sheep, one thousand cattle and abundant harvests. In the third year we had a surplus of produce and wool, forty thousand sheep, twenty thousand cattle and with the help of irrigation abundant harvest. In the fourth year, in addition to two hundred thousand sheep, seventy-five thousand cattle and abundant harvests, we have added a woolen mill, in which we manufacture our own woolen blankets and yarn and knit our own woolen stockings and shirts. We can sell these in any market. We are now building another mill and will work our wool product into cloth. You ask how we have progressed so rapidly? I reply that the Brotherhood throughout the United States has contributed much to our enterprise by purchasing our surplus products and disposing of them in eastern markets. But better than this we have never lost the labor power of one able-bodied man during all this time. The confidence of the Brotherhood in us was due to the magnificent generalship of one great man, and that one great man was and is John Thompson of Co-opolis. (Here the enthusiasm became unbounded and the audience cheered for several minutes.)

"But, my friends, let me say to you that John Thompson has not only been a general. He inherited a large fortune from his father and while he has not contributed one cent of this to the Commonwealth he has sent men at his expense to several of the great cities of this country to search out deserving persons and has advanced to them the funds to come hither and to pay the one hundred dollars required of each person on admission. These amounts have been repaid from the wages of the recipient in due time. I say to you, gentlemen, that this world does not contain a more thoughtful, able and public-spirited man than John Thompson, whom I now nominate for governor of Idaho."

Mr. Edmunds sat down and the great hall fairly shook with the applause which, as often as it subsided, was repeated again and again. James Rutherford of Boise City, a delegate who, although a member of the National Brotherhood, was, as yet, not connected with any colony, seconded the nomination and moved that President Thompson be declared the nominee by acclamation. The motion was put and carried without a dissenting vote amid the wildest enthusiasm. The nominee having been escorted to the platform by a committee designated for that purpose, addressed the convention, after the tremendous cheers given in his honor had subsided.

As he stood facing the great audience waiting an opportunity to begin I thought I had never seen him look so masterful before. His tall, powerfully built frame presented the picture of an athlete, and his face expressed an intelligence which could only belong to a man of great intellectual force. He was the personification of strength of physique, mind and will. His face, as usual, was clean shaven, his black hair was combed straight back from his forehead, his large dark eyes surveyed his audience with a look which was a strange commingling of love and command. I do not believe a man, friend or enemy, in the multitude before him doubted his sincerity, or was conscious, for the moment, of any other sentiment than that of admiration. He drew all men toward him and, as many have often related to me since, when they came within his influence they seemed most naturally to fall in line behind him and acknowledge him as leader. He began to speak slowly, but his voice could be heard distinctly throughout the great hall.

"Mr. President and gentlemen," said he, "we have now reached a point in the history of this Commonwealth which marks the beginning of an epoch. To my mind it is apparent that all the events of christian civilization have been a preparation for the higher civilization which we are privileged to usher in. It has been said that 'Time's noblest offspring is her last,' and we may hope that such offspring is this day born, and that it will thrive and continue to grow until time shall be no more. I have always believed that the old system from which we have sought to escape is barbaric feudalism, and that, whether in its ancient **military or its** modern commercial form, it was distorted by selfishness and greed.

"The motives of the robber baron **of the** dark ages and the self-serving organizer of trusts to-day do not differ, and if in the dark ages **the** one, by force of arms, held possession of fertile valleys and exacted tribute from neighboring peoples, the other by fraud monopolizes an industry **and** seeks to crush out all competitors. Death strewed the paths of both, the one being no less hideous in blood than the other was in the gaunt and shrunken spectre of starvation. The one, however, spent itself in its own terrors and disappeared before the awful ravages of destructive **war.** So the other has exhausted itself in greed and making **the** automaton serve in **the stead of** man has taught man the lesson **of** co-operation.

"I have never been a **friend** to political socialism as **a** factor in building up **the** Co-operative Commonwealth. My judgment has proposed to me the development of the co-operative principle in commercial and industrial lines until it became so strong that it could not be ignored. In that manner the railroads, telegraphs and other vast interests from unknown forces, developed into those mighty giants which **came to control** the government and now terrorize the people. I have hoped that the Co-operative Commonwealth developing in like manner, slowly but surely, might with very different motives and **for** different purposes, become strong enough to **take the** government and wield it for the common good of all. If I mistake not, the time **has come, the** Commonwealth is equal to its purpose, **and** we may assume our political rights. If we win in the election now approaching the state of Idaho will become a co-operative state. Our **aim** should be to establish our system without encroaching upon the constitution of the nation. We will violate none of the provisions of that instrument, but we will carefully observe all its limitations. This will be no more difficult for us than it is for the great trusts and monopolies, which have become so powerful that they are able to obtain an interpretation of the constitution when they wish it, whereby its limits have been and are constantly extended to suit their purposes. By presenting a model of one co-operative commonwealth, we may, and I believe will, sooner or later induce other states to follow our lead, and the entire sisterhood of states may form one great co-operative nation. But we should advance to the accomplishment of our purpose, in this state, with wisdom and caution.

"We must make as few mistakes as possible. Our endeavor must be to understand and strictly conform to the law. We must respect the opinions of those who do not agree with us. We must not disturb any citizen in the enjoyment of his property and it should never be forgotten that the Commonwealth depends for its growth solely upon volunteers. You have, my friends, nominated me to be the first governor of Co-operative Idaho. I have consented to accept this dignity only because I now believe that he who acts as President of the Co-operative Commonwealth should also be the governor of the state, until every vestige of the old system is removed from Idaho and all its people have voluntarily entered the new system. We must have a dual government, but the Co-operative Commonwealth must control it.

"Idaho, the name of our state, is said to mean 'Light on the Mountains.' We will strive to give it a still broader signification and, God willing, it shall be a light to all the people.

"The Co-operative Commonwealth was conceived by men who believed the human race capable of advancing to the highest ideal of civilization. It never depended, for its success, upon those philosophers who chose to believe that because they themselves did not feel the pinch of want therefore none others need feel it, nor of those philanthropists who were always going about giving that sort of temporary relief which only served to make the source of poverty all the more prolific and the cause all the more obscure. They did not ask advice of learned students of history, who by that dim light discovered only the passions and sins of great sinners, and being diverted by the monsters whose careers filled the world with their unhallowed fame, failed to observe the patient, law-abiding, industrious and sober millions who toiled unobserved in the background.

"The Co-operative Commonwealth is founded upon the theory that all men can as well habituate themselves to conform to higher as to lower standards. The individualist, the theoretical democrat, urges that our system will tend to destroy self-reliance and to weaken the individual man. The same proposition carried to its logical conclusion would abolish all co-operative effort, and as society, even in its lowest forms, rests upon co-operation, all society is, if judged by that standard, but weakening in its effects. But whether co-operation makes men weak depends upon its purpose. If it is organized for theft, murder or lewdness, then it certainly tends to make men morally weak. If it is organized for luxury, riot or intemperance, then it tends to make them physically weak. If its purpose is blasphemy, gross materialism and the prevention of the free investigation of religious truth, it cannot fail to make men spiritually weak. The Co-operative Commonwealth is organized for none of these. Its aim is to produce a better and stronger man mentally, physically, morally and spiritually. It gives the fullest education to all and endeavors to make the minds of its pupils independent and self-reliant. It offers the largest opportunity for physical culture, and in all moral and spiritual spheres presents the highest and best standards, without limiting freedom of thought or criticism.

"In brief, the consummation of our programme is, the complete elimination of speculation, gambling and unjust advantage from the social state, and to guarantee our members the rewards of their own efforts. We do not permit the rich to rob the poor, the strong to prey upon the weak, nor the keen to sharpen their faculties at the material expense of those who may be dull. To say that this is injurious to the development of what is best in man, is to assert that life has no purpose except physical gain, and that the main purpose of life is to provide clothing, shelter and food. We hold that these are only the means **of life** and that the purpose of life is the highest development of manhood and **womanhood for** the acquisition and appreciation of truth.

"The Co-operative Commonwealth is a great insurance association, and as such guarantees to its member the enjoyment of his or her earnings. It goes one step further, and assures him **that** if accident or sickness shall **deprive him** of physical or mental ability, or death shall remove him from a dependent family, all physical and mental needs shall be provided for him or them. All such advantages were and are regarded as lending strength to any form of society and surely they cannot be other than meritorious features of our system.

With a firm belief in the righteousness of **our great cause,** and assuring you that my life is devoted to your **service, I** again express my willingness to accept this **nomination.** I need give you but one pledge and giving that you **can feel** perfectly secure that **your** will is to govern the **future.** It is my purpose **to use** my utmost endeavors to **have a constitutional** convention called **as** speedily as possible, **if I shall be** elected, and through that convention you, **my brothers,** will establish **the** Co-operative Commonwealth **forever."**

Again the convention went wild with enthusiasm and the delegates and visitors crowded around the nominee. I have attended many state conventions, but never before saw one which resembled so closely in its magnitude and tumultuous enthusiasm those assemblages in which the national parties are wont to designate their choice for chief magistrate of the great republic. The reason, however, was apparent. All understood that this convention was to initiate a peaceful revolution whose influence would ultimately be world-wide in extent.

After the enthusiasm attending the nomination had subsided the convention nominated the remainder of the ticket. **All the** candidates were co-operators, but selected from different localities.

For Secretary of State, Addison **Wellman of** Boise City; State Treasurer, Benjamin D. **Corwin of Al**pha, then a flourishing colony, now **a** great city, on the Snake river, about sixty miles from Co-opolis. For Lieutenant-Governor, Edward J. Murphy of Banford, in the northern part of the state. This ticket, **be it** said, did not fully conform to our plan to have the officers **of** the state and the association identical, but it was considered best to unite all our colonies under one brotherhood government within the state **and** then to carry our plan of official identity of state **and** brotherhood into effect. The platform adopted was **very** brief. It pledged the Co-operative Commonwealth to respect all vested rights and to conform to the constitution of the United States, but asserted that the sources and machinery of material production should be owned in common. It also declared for **a** constitutional convention to be called at an early **date.**

CHAPTER IX.

MY HOME LIFE—AUNT LYDIA—MISS WOODBERRY—TRIP TO CANYON LAKE.

According to the laws of the Brotherhood each company was entitled to a fortnightly holiday and as far as possible work was entirely suspended on Sunday. The day after the convention was Thursday and the company of which I was a member enjoyed a "lay-off" on that day. Although the convention had kept me up late the night before I arose early, having arranged an outing in the country with a small company of friends. The Co-opolitan lay on the walk as I stepped out to sit upon the veranda while breakfast was being prepared. I picked it up and sitting down proceeded to read the news. At that time my residence was on Salem Avenue where it widened into an extensive park in which was a lake fed from an artesian well around which a grove of young trees grew luxuriantly. My house was not a large one. It had been constructed for me by the association, as all private dwellings had been for their occupants, upon a plan such as the occupant furnished. The estimated cost to the Association was one thousand dollars as represented by orders paid out by it for the labor and material used. It is well to state here that the construction of a house was to the Association hardly more than a question of labor. My house was, like all the dwellings in the city at that time except apartment houses, a frame structure. The timber had been obtained from the neighboring forests by our own people without cost. It had been sawed into lumber by our mills. It had been put together by our carpenters. The stone for the foundations, the lime for the walls and ceiling, the brick, mortar, sand, and, in short, all but the nails, screws, locks and gears were produced by the labor of our own people. Three years later, even these were manufactured in Idaho. So that the house cost little more than the cost of the labor employed in its construction. But it was, nevertheless, as well built and as commodious as one costing three thousand dollars in an eastern city under the competitive system, showing that our co-operative system was at least three times as effective in this line as the competitive system. This showing, however, is limited to the building trades alone, and does not include the enormous increase of productivity by the employment of all labor power in the direction of greatest utility.

The rooms were all provided with open fireplaces for heating purposes, but the cooking apparatus consisted of a gas stove. Gas, electricity, steam heating and both hot and cold water were furnished by the Association at a small cost. In fact the rent of the house, its lighting and heating as well as its supply of water, cost me only one hundred and forty-four dollars per year, or twelve dollars per month, and the service was complete. Besides this, any repairs needed were attended to at once and the house was kept in perfect order. The furniture was also provided by the department store as selected by myself. Even the carpets were manufactured in Co-opolis. This furniture was paid for by me in Commonwealth orders and was mine without reservation.

In those times most of us preferred to prepare our breakfasts at home, but we usually either had our other meals sent from the public kitchens close at hand or went to the public dining halls or hotel. The Domestic department had charge of the entire domestic work of the city and companies were stationed in each precinct for that purpose. Whenever any house wanted domestic work performed it was only necessary to telephone to the proper station and a well-trained domestic, either man or woman, as desired, was sent for the purpose. The time of the domestic was charged to the house and the cost of the service collected by the department each month, like the rent, gas, telephone, water and heating bills. The streets and grounds were kept in order by the city at the public expense.

For nearly a year an aunt of mine, an old widow of most excellent character, had been keeping house for me. She was not a member of the association, did no service and drew no pay, but lived entirely on my bounty. She was a strict Congregationalist of the New England type, read her bible diligently, assisted in maintaining a religious society of that denomination, and was one of the most kindly and lovable souls in our neighborhood. She was, of course too old to become an active member of the society and too poor to purchase a membership. She did not altogether approve the system in operation in Co-opolis, but rarely ever expressed any criticism upon it.

I think she was as comfortable and happy as any old lady in the country, for her time was employed, either in sewing light domestic work, reading, writing letters home, or riding with the motorcycle which I kept at her disposal. She was always endeavoring to economize in household matters because she felt that she was a charge upon me. It was in vain that I assured her of the growing wealth of Co-opolis, and tried to get her to realize that I had a share in all this wealth which would last me my lifetime. She could not comprehend it and still continued to save.

This morning she was quite busy, according to her usual custom, and it was not long after I sat down to read that her cheerful voice called me to partake of the morning meal. It was not an elaborate one, but it was an Idaho production almost entirely. The rolled oats were grown, rolled and prepared in Co-opolis; the flour, maple syrup, butter and even the sugar were made in Idaho, and none better were ever made elsewhere. The sugar was the product of the beet-sugar factory at Laselle, which had been established by the National Brotherhood two years before. The salt was manufactured by our Association, and this morning we had plates which were among the first productions of a new industry added by the Department of Manufactures just two months previously. The silver on the table was some which I had inherited from my mother and was highly prized. The oak extension table, sideboard and chairs in the dining room also represented our Co-opolitan labor. Aunt Lydia sat at the table with me and served the coffee.

"Willie," said she, as she reached me the cream, "I guess I won't go to-day. I promised Mrs. Cressy that I would spend a day with her, and she has a holiday; so, if you have no objection, I will go there instead of the lake."

"Why, Aunt Lydia," I exclaimed, "what has made you change so suddenly? Of course you must go with us. Mr. Fuller and Joe Preston are all going and if you don't go I'll simply have to ride alone. You must go."

"No, Willie." She always called me Willie. "No," she declared again. "The Prestons have company just from Boston, a Miss Woodberry; I met her yesterday. She seems to be a very nice young lady and I want you to go with her and show her the valley."

"Why, aunt," I replied, "I will do nothing of the kind. I want you to go and have made my arrangements accordingly."

But my aunt was obdurate and all I could say was unavailing. The truth was she was anxious that I should marry and was, very much to my annoyance at times, always contriving to throw me in the way of young ladies, hoping that I would meet my fate. I suspected that this was another scheme of that kind and felt provoked. If I could have found a good excuse I would have canceled my engagement and remained at home. But no excuse presented itself. What was even worse, as I thought, my aunt had gone so far as to invite Miss Woodberry to take her place in the party, which that young lady as a guest of the Prestons, who were also going, very naturally and promptly accepted. Of course I could not scold the dear old meddling lady, and so, although much put out, I philosophically submitted to the inevitable.

After breakfast Joe Preston, a young man about twenty, who had just entered the Industrial Army, in the Transportation department, but who had a holiday also, came over and said that he had been to the precinct kitchen and had all the edibles put up for the trip and that Miss Woodberry was ready to go whenever I was. He took the motorcycle from the shed back of the house, adjusted the storage battery, and conducted the vehicle around to the front door. I entered and a minute later we were at the door of the Preston cottage, where we found the entire party, Miss Woodberry among the rest, waiting with their vehicles. The formalities of an introduction over I assisted Miss Woodberry to her place and seating myself by her side we started away, the rest of the party following.

Our destination was the lake made by damming the waters of Deer River and flowing about two hundred acres of land in the canyon where the stream emerges from the mountains. We called it Canyon Lake and laid out a park around it, which at that time was not completed, but gave promise of much beauty. It was my intention to ascend the divide south of the city, pursue the road which ran along the slope and take in the scenery which delighted the eye from that elevation. So we followed the asphalt pavement as far as it went in that direction and then rolled along the smoothly macadamized country driveway. The Co-opolitans of that day were very proud of their roads and spent much time and labor upon them. They were all wide, smooth and well shaded and accommodations for drinking both for man and beast—horses were still in use for drawing heavy burdens at that time—were provided from the big flume and the reservoirs of our system of irrigation.

The lady by my side was enthusiastic over all she saw and so bright and unaffected were her remarks and exclamations that, before we had gone very far, I began to enjoy her society. She was not a remarkably handsome person, but she had what I suppose my female acquaintances would call "style." That, of course, was a matter of dress, all of which had its effect on me as fashion intended, but none of which I could describe. In a general way I could see that she had a jaunty hat full of bright-colored artificial flowers, a **loose-fitting white waist and a** gown **of** some blue material. Her form was' tall and rather slender, her hair **auburn, her** features somewhat pronounced, **but** intellectual, **her** mouth indicated firmness, but was in an everlasting conspiracy with a pair of large blue eyes to ex**press** all that **is** bright and sunny in the feminine character.

She had one of those faces, in **which** no **feature was above criticism,** but upon which **so many** happy thoughts and kindly emotions were continually expressing themselves, that criticism was as soon forgotten as made, and once forgotten was never recalled. I was seized, as we walked together, with a great desire to show her novel or beautiful scenes, and to tell her what I knew. I never enjoyed anything so much as the varying expressions of her face, always intelligent, always pure, always gentle, and withal full of strong character. It was evident that she had read much, **seen many** places and had a clear understanding. But it was also apparent that she was in search of **the** pure, the beautiful, the good, and she was altogether like what she sought. One most remarkable fact about her was that although a Bostonian she did not insist that Boston should be the sole subject of conversation.

After an hour's journey from the city, moving rapidly along the levels, swiftly down the inclines and slowly up the steep road which ascended to the divide, we reached the place which I have always considered the best from which to view Co-opolis. Here our party halted for a time, remaining in our carriages and discussing the many objects of interest. The mountains, black and threatening, looked down upon us as if with sullen displeasure, and beyond the wild wastes of treeless and houseless valleys, far to the south, rose the weird forms of the Seven Devils, presiding over a kind of a golden Hades. **But it was not** the mountains nor the wilderness which attracted us mostly.

Before us lay the garden of brotherly **love,** in whose bosom nestled the fair city of Co-opolis. That city was indeed a picture of peace and loveliness, with all **its** great public buildings, its wide streets, its artificial lakes and magnificent urban parks. I pointed out the buildings and parks to my lady companion and took much pleasure in giving her brief historical sketches of several of them. But even Co-opolis, with all its artificial beauty, was not the greatest object of interest. The valley itself, subjected to the most thorough cultivation to which the most approved methods could reduce it, lay before us "as fair as the garden of the gods upon the slopes of Eden." Directing our attention to the north we saw the silvery expanse of Canyon Lake glistening in the sun. Along both the northern and southern slopes of the valley extended the finely constructed ditches and flumes conducting the waters of the lake to many different reservoirs, where they were stored and distributed when occasion demanded.

I explained, what was a fact, that the rainfall in this region had increased to such an extent since the valley became inhabited and cultivated that for two years the supply of water had been comparatively little used in irrigation. But irrigation assured us our crops and there was no danger that a drought would ever destroy them. Eighty thousand acres constituted our cultivated farm. I pointed out the apple, peach and pear orchards and vineyards and spoke of the promise these orchards and vineyards gave of a large supply of fruit in perhaps another year. I showed the corn, wheat and potato fields, the vegetable gardens and the extensive hothouses, and explained that at times three thousand members of our Industrial Army were engaged on the farm.

We could also see the numerous sheds constructed in sheltered places, for the sheep and cattle which our shepherds and herders attended on the ranges, and the large barns here and there in which the harvests were stored and kept. The fields and ranges had produced in the last two years an enormous surplus. This surplus, however, the Brotherhood in the nation had taken or it had been distributed at the instance of the Brotherhood among the new colonies which it had established throughout the state.

My companion asked me the **wealth of the** colony, **and** my answer was that its buildings could **not** be constructed **in** any competitive eastern city for less than $15,000,000.00, but **that** they probably cost an amount of labor estimated by our standards at $4,500,000.00. The 80,000 acres of land, to which the Association had title, were worth $50.00 per acre at least, or $4,000,000.00. **The** personal property, consisting of machinery, stocks **of** goods, sheep, cattle, horses, wagons, tricycles, bicycles, motorcycles and farm products, were worth $8,500,000.00 and the water right, irrigating ditches, electric railroads, gas and electric plants, water system **for** the city, heating system and **public** utilities which brought or could be made to bring **a** revenue, were produced **by** the labor of the Industrial Army, without an **outlay** of much cash, and were worth at least **$5,500,-000.00.** All **this has** been created by labor in **five** years, and, **of course,** the value of the city lots is not estimated.

Yet the **mere** fact that 15,000 people lived **on** these lots was sufficient to give them an enormous value if they **were** to be sold for cash. Indeed, **I** think the lots in the city at that time were worth $4,000,000.00 **as an** investment, based upon their rental values.

We continued our observation **of the** valley in this manner for about half an **hour and then** rather reluctantly moved on. The day was spent **pleasantly,** in fishing, sailing and picnicking. There was **at the lake** an Association restaurant where, in the summer time, fish dinners were made a specialty. Special attention was given to supplying our city with fresh fish and a large fish hatchery was also located here. The **event of** the day, however, was the observation of the scenery from the divide both on the trip to and the trip from the lake, for **we** again stopped on our return and again feasted upon that vision of fertility and abundance.

When we arrived **home that** evening we were still intent on the **full** enjoyment of our holiday, and, as the great French tragedienne, with a superb company, had been engaged for the week by the Association, we went to the theater. Here, again, Aunt Lydia, having an aversion for theatrical performances, which New England Congregationalism had instilled into her, preferred to remain at home, and I was once more obliged to accompany my new-found friend Miss Woodberry. I may say, however, that whatever my aunt's aversion to the theater may have been I did not share it and the aversion which I felt in the morning to leaving my good, old aunt at home was not so keenly felt in the evening.

CHAPTER X.

THE CAMPAIGN OF 1902—DRIVING CAPITAL FROM THE STATE—THE POLITICAL MINISTER—VICTORY.

The political campaign of 1902 in Idaho was one of the most notable ever waged in the United States. It was interesting to the entire country because it was understood that if the Co-operative Commonwealth was victorious the changes which would be effected in the government, laws and industrial system of the state would be radical and sweeping. The moneyed interests all over the country were alarmed, but it may be said that in those times the "moneyed interests" were always in a state of alarm at every suggestion of a reform which proposed the betterment of the condition of the masses.

As a result of this "alarm" a system of colonization in Idaho was begun with a view to outvoting the co-operators on election day. But the extent of the Brotherhood of the Co-operative Comonwealth was little understood by the business and moneyed interests of the nation. They supposed it to be practically confined to Idaho when in truth it had its branches throughout the entire country.. The effort to colonize voters in Idaho was rendered abortive except in the mining regions of the northern part of the state, and even there the colonizers were not as successful as they supposed. The Brotherhood, secretly giving the most useful aid to co-operators, caused many ardent friends to be enlisted as colonists of the enemy, and these, immediately on arrival in Idaho, communicated with our leaders and we were kept constantly informed as to the movements of the opposition.

The Brotherhood numbered one million members outside of Idaho and if we had asked them to contribute to our financial strength they could and would have sent us from one to five million dollars. This, however, was deemed unnecessary, and we confined our expenditures to the education of the masses with regard to our purposes, and the prevention of the gross frauds which we expected the opposition to perpetrate. Great speakers of national fame were sent from all parts of the country to discuss the issues of this campaign. Competition and co-operation had here locked horns and this tremendous issue was to be fought out once for all.

The principal argument made by the opposition was that the success of co-operation, besides destroying personal liberty, would drive out all the capital in the state, and all the capital approaching the state away from it. To this position, which was depicted on every opposition stump, our great leader, President Thompson, always made but one reply.

"Drive capital from the state!" exclaimed he. "Prevent its entrance! Why! Let them take every dollar of gold and silver and every item of what they call credit away forever. Let them leave us the land and ability to labor and we will speedily reverse the order. Instead of Idaho being a suppliant at the door of capital, we shall soon see capital, so boastful and arrogant now, an abject suppliant at the door of Idaho.

"Instead of capital directing industry we shall find industry directing and controlling capital. But how will they withdraw capital? Will they fill up the mines they have dug? Will they tear up the rails they have laid? Will they stop their trains on the boundary line or rush through without stopping? Will they transport the houses and farms on which they hold mortgages? They can, of course, do none of these things, nor do they contemplate it. But they say we intend to repudiate our indebtedness to them. In the great record of the Omniscient Lawgiver, in which the list of those moral obligations which ought to be kept are found, it is not probable that all the debts of the people are numbered, but into that we shall never inquire. All moral and legal obligations which rest upon it shall be strictly and fully paid."

The fight waxed warmer as election day approached. Every effort was made to stir up the basest passions against the Co-operative Commonwealth. We heard of a riot and what amounted almost to a pitched battle in the mining regions of the Coeur d'Alene Mountains, and learned, to our surprise, that we had a large number of adherents among the Trade Unionists and the Miners' Unions of that section. An equally great surprise was that, although our movement was in no sense hostile to any church, and as a matter of fact encouraged all religious denominations in their work, the ministers of the gospel were, as a rule, among our most bitter opponents and, excepting those who presided over co-operators of their own denominations, they were disposed to denounce us as opposed to morals. I regret to say that from this class of campaign speakers and political workers came the most outrageous misrepresentations of the campaign.

I beg to be understood aright. I make no charge against the church, or against ministers. God knows that I have the highest regard for both, but I have noticed not only in connection with the campaign of 1902 but other great campaigns before and since that when they step out of their true sphere into politics these amiable, innocent and estimable gentlemen generally become the catspaws of the most unscrupulous political monkeys. They are undeniably caught by men who make the loudest professions of honesty, justice and virtue, when in truth those who proclaim their merits in these regards with the greatest vigor are not necessarily the most sincere or deserving. Vigor of tongue does not always indicate a healthy conscience, but it generally catches the political minister.

The day before election Thompson and I met at the Co-opolitan. The work of the campaign was now practically completed as far as speaking was concerned. Thompson had certainly done his duty, for he had spoken in every county seat and every considerable town in the state.

Everywhere he had been welcomed by great crowds and everywhere it had been acknowledged that he was a man of commanding genius. Indeed, all this was conceded by the newspaper press throughout the Union. But he told me confidentially that he did not trust the appearances which seemed so flattering and cited several instances to show the uncertainty of political events. I was a younger man and my enthusiasm caused me to entertain no doubt of the complete success of our entire programme.

Election day passed off without incident. The vote was heavy. Every woman of voting age, as well as every man, voted, and the vote cast was more than twice as large as the state had ever cast in any previous election, the grand total being 190,000. Of these our ticket received 115,000, giving us a majority of 40,000. We had elected more than two-thirds of both houses of the legislature and the victory for the Co-operative Commonwealth was complete.

How we shouted, and went nearly mad with joy in Co-opolis. The total vote of our city, numbering 6,661, had been cast for the entire ticket. I have not mentioned the fact that in the distribution of political honors I had received the nomination, equivalent to election, for state senator, and I may now say that I was unanimously elected.

I did not vote for myself.

I was the only candidate. When the result of the election was known we appointed the following evening for a grand jollification. It was an occasion to be remembered. The army, 7,000 strong, not all residents of Co-opolis, as some were permanently stationed in the country, marched through the streets, with music furnished by the city band. This band consisted of one hundred first-class musicians, and was one of the best in the entire western country. There were other amateur bands which were drilled to a high degree of excellence, and the army marched to such music. There was a grand illumination in the evening, and a magnificent display of fireworks.

CHAPTER XI.

THE BROTHERHOOD CONVEYS ITS IDAHO POSSESSIONS TO THE CO-OPOLITAN ASSOCIATION — ARRANGEMENTS FOR COLONISTS — TYPICAL INSTANCES — JARVIS RICHARDSON—MRS. ELIZABETH MAXON.

The National Brotherhood of the Co-operative Commonwealth had prior to the election of 1902, in a delegate convention held in Chicago, passed a resolution approving the Co-opolitan system of co-operation and directing that all colonies and colonists entering Idaho, under its auspices, after January 1st, 1903, enter and become merged in Colony Number One, as Co-opolis was named in the Brotherhood records. It also transferred all its property, including the beet-sugar factory at Laselle, a gold mine at Banford, in the Coeur d'Alene Mountains, and several large tracts of land and small colonies to us, upon the theory that we were better able to superintend the details of state building, while the Brotherhood should simply aid us with funds to extend our good works, furnish us with colonists and distribute our surplus product.

Our Legislation Council, anticipating large accessions to our population on this account, was in constant session and during the entire winter of 1902-3 large plans were under consideration for the utilization of the new labor power. The National Brotherhood had contracted not to send us more than 10,000 new members during the year 1903 and to pay us $1,000,000.00 cash or one hundred dollars for each person sent for our surplus products stored in various barns and storehouses.

It was not considered that these new colonists should all remain in Co-opolis. About two thousand of them were to be retained in certain productive lines in which we were already prepared to set them at work. One of these was a large woolen mill located down the stream toward Snake River, capable of employing one thousand hands. We had a large quantity of wool on hand, and were ready to take all which was offered in exchange for goods at the department store. It was also agreed between the National Brotherhood and our council that they should send us one thousand persons skilled in the manufacture of woolen fabrics. These we agreed to receive on equal terms with all other members. We also arranged for the establishment of a large boot and shoe factory, an extensive fruit and vegetable canning factory, and another one still for the slaughtering, dressing, preparing and packing of pork, beef and other meats. The slaughter houses were designed to be situated about six miles from Co-opolis over the divide on the Seven Devils branch of the Oregon Short Line. These skilled artisans numbered in all about three thousand. The rest, consisting of six thousand adults, were to enter the Industrial Army as common workers.

We estimated that we could employ this new industrial army in opening up another large valley in the same county fifteen miles south of Co-opolis. That valley was in nearly all respects similar to Deer Valley, except that it was larger and the divides and tables were covered with a thick growth of timber. We considered that it was proper to retain about half of the seven thousand new men to work in and about Co-opolis and to send an equal number of our older members to the new fields. The plan was, first of all, to provide irrigation; second, to break thirty thousand acres of land and seed it to corn; third, to construct buildings sufficiently commodious to house the companies of the Industrial Army which might be necessary to make the valley productive and protect its structures and products from destruction. It was then intended to be a sort of an industrial outpost for Co-opolis, and was placed in charge of the Agricultural department.

When the new colonists began to arrive in large numbers the scene presented in the main hall of the building was interesting. The department chiefs took turns presiding at the hearing of applications for membership. I remember very well my own experience one day the latter part of January. I had obtained a temporary leave of absence from the senate in order to assume the duties as chief of my department. There were eight hundred newcomers, men and women. Each was sworn to answer truly all questions put touching his or her age, education, trade or calling, nationality, former place of residence, family and career. His application, together with certificates of medical examiners, was examined and if approved by the National Brotherhood the following contract was handed him for his signature: "It is hereby agreed by and between Peter Jones, party of the first part, and Colony Number One of the Co-operative Commonwealth known as the Co-opolitan Association, party of the second part, that in consideration of the promises, agreements and undertakings hereinafter set forth, said first party enters the employ of said second party as a laborer for the term of three years. That he agrees to do and perform any and all work which said second party shall require of him in any part of the state of Idaho to the best of his ability. That he agrees to conform to all the rules, regulations and laws which are now in force or shall become in force in or in connection with said colony, provided the same do not impair the obligation hereof. Said second party agrees to pay said first party for said service in the products of labor on hand or obtainable by said second party, an amount equal to forty per cent of the yearly product of the labor of said colony divided by the total number of members of said colony above the age of twenty years, less fines and forfeitures, the same to be paid in such amounts, and at such times, within each year, as shall be provided by the Legislative Council of said second party."

The examination to which applicants were subjected is well illustrated by the record of one who has since become one of the famous Industrial chiefs of the state.

"What is your name, age, occupation and place of residence?" asked I of a medium-sized man with a strong, square face, and a large forehead, who arose and held up his right hand to take the oath.

"Name, Jarvis Richardson.. Age, thirty years. Occupation, printer. Former residence, St. Paul, Minnesota."

"Name of former employer and when last employed."

"Pioneer Press Publishing Company. Was laid off three years ago."

"Reason for discharge?"

"Improved typesetting machines."

"Do you understand and favor co-operation, or are you desirous of entering the Brotherhood for temporary protection?"

"I believe I understand the principle and purpose of co-operation. Having been excluded from usefulness in my own trade by the introduction of labor-saving devices, I realize that an injustice has been done me. I should have had the benefit of the labor-saving device, but instead of that I am simply supplanted by an automaton. The machine which excluded me from my place and has kept me comparatively idle ever since does the work which it formerly took five men to do. If the same results were accomplished, as it ultimately will be, in all departments four-fifths of the labor of human beings would be thrown aside and four-fifths of the laborers would starve. This would curtail the consumption of products of such machinery, and a portion of those who operate them would then be discharged on the plea of hard times, limited demand and overproduction.

"The industrial system now in operation throughout the Christian world was devised for an ignorant and barbarous people. Invention, learning, industry and progress are showing its entire inefficiency. Learning must be limited to a few if that system is to live. Under it, if industry produces enough for all, stagnation results, because that system makes no provision for wise and equitable distribution. Progress is impossible because it strains society to a point of revolution and destruction follows. The co-operative system, on the contrary, deems labor-saving machinery a blessing, and its adoption simply increases production and is a relief and benefit to the laborer. It does not diminish his share of the product, but reduces his hours of labor. You cannot have too much education and learning in the co-operative system because all are educated, and yet each is required to submit to his share of labor and drudging. This tends to destroy false pride, and prevent vanity. Moreover, men come to realize their true relation to one another.

"Industry can never cause overproduction in the co-operative system. If too much is produced for the members to consume they do not therefore find it necessary to starve a portion of their number. Such a condition is hurtful to none. The co-operative system demands progress. Every step forward brings a reward and does not suggest a danger. Every advance is a blessing not to a few, but to all. A system which is large enough, just enough and expansive enough to admit of the unfoldment of all the powers and virtues of the race cannot be less than Christian."

The manner of the applicant as he expressed himself was that of a polished and educated gentleman. It was not customary for us to encourage lengthy speeches on the part of applicants, during the year 1903 nor the years following, but once in a while a man of commanding will and intellect would challenge our attention and we would listen to him as I did to Mr. Richardson. He was a sufferer from one cause, and understood the cause and its only cure far better than a philosopher who only observes and could not feel the condition it imposed on him.

"It is claimed that the individual is weakened and made dependent by our system, Mr. Richardson," said I. "The claim is also made that the man who escapes the perils of the industrial system comes out with a stronger character and a more independent manhood than if such perils had not been encountered. Have you a different opinion?"

"I do not know," was the reply, "how great a manhood your system will develop. It teaches, however, the lesson of brotherhood, **and gives me** protection for my wife and babies **by furnishing me** an opportunity to be industrious. The **competitive system** might **not be** objectionable if it would **do the same.** But it does not permit fair competition. **It demands that a man be industrious,** but gives him **no chance to work. It permits a few to** monopolize **land, water, power, money and all the sources,** means and machinery **of production, and then asks the** disinherited **and landless ones to compete when competition** is impossible.

"The system called competitive is not competitive. It is a system whereby a favored few are permitted to rob the many. As for the perils of that system developing character, I admit they do. The most remarkable character and those most admired in **it are the** modern Shylocks. If that sort of character is desirable, then the system is a success, but I do not covet its benefits. It seems to me the perils of savagery are much **more** effective to bring out strong traits of character **and build** up a manhood more courageous, self-reliant, and even heroic, certainly **not more** brutal, than the trading, cozzening, cheating, gambling, sordid methods which make up this so-called 'Competitive System.'"

It was not possible for **me** in the press of business **to continue the conversation** further that day. Indeed, the arguments offered by the applicant were not new to me, and it was only because of **the** strong individuality **of** the man that I stopped **to converse** with him at all. It was, however, a part of **my business** to investigate the qualifications **of applicants and when they** had been accepted to enroll **them in the** proper department. Each department had its **enrolling** clerk present, who received the signature of **the new member in** the department **to** which he was assigned. A **few formal** questions more were put to Mr. Richardson and I assigned **him to** the Messenger and Publishing department, where **a** vacancy **had** occurred within **a** week by the death of a trusted member.

He of course entered as a mere printer, being compelled **to earn** promotion by the efficiency of his work.

The examination **and** acceptance of applicants went on with great rapidity after this, and no incident occurred worthy of note until after the noon lunch. A woman about thirty-six years old presented her application. After the usual formal questions I asked:

"Are you married?"

"I am a widow," she answered; "my husband was killed in a railroad collision five years ago."

"Have you children?"

"I have seven—three boys and four girls."

"Have you them with you?"

"All are here. Mr. Thompson advised me to come and make this application, so I have been saving up all my money and I am here."

"You say you live in Boise? You are not recommended by the Brotherhood. Have you any recommendations?"

"I have one from Mr. Thompson." Here she handed me a note from our President, now Governor of the state, and upon reading it I found that she was an intelligent and deserving woman who was anxious to educate her children. She had saved, through several years' hard work at the washtub and in various kinds of domestic work, the fee necessary to enter the colony, and, although it was her all, she was ready to pay it for such a purpose.

"What shall I do for a home?" she asked.

"We have excellent houses, in one of which you shall live," I replied.

"Can I send my children to school?" she continued.

"You are required to do so. Education is compulsory. Your children will be turned over to the Department of Education."

"Am I to be separated from them?"

"You and they will live together in the same house."

"But I am a member of the Episcopal church. I desire my children brought up in that church."

"The religious education of your children is your own care. Send them to what church you will. Episcopal, Methodist, Baptist, Catholic, Congregationalist and other denominations are represented here."

"Would it be wrong for me to ask how much my wages are to be?"

"You will receive checks or orders the first year entitling you to one-third as much as a skilled first-year member. The second year you will receive as much as any other member of the Industrial Army, skilled or unskilled, officer or private. Last year each member received $1,200.00 in orders or checks entitling him to the use of public conveyances, railroads, house, water, gas, light, heat and other public utility, to goods, wares and merchandise, meals at restaurant or hotel, to admission to entertainments, use of public ovens, and, in short, whatever you need. If your children are infants the Department of Education has trained nurses to care for them. If a mother is nursing her babe we give her a furlough until the period of nursing ceases, but her pay continues. We encourage the mother to be with her children as much as possible, as we believe a mother's love is one of the influences, under proper conditions, which inspire purity and develop manhood and womanhood in the child."

"But if I must work I cannot care for my children and get them ready for school in the morning."

"Women who have children are placed, as far as possible, in companies which do their work during what are called school hours. You will be assigned to the Domestic department and its officers will place you where you belong. You will go to your work at 9 o'clock and continue until 12. You will then take an hour for your own lunch and returning to work continue until 5."

I felt great satisfaction at being able to give this poor woman information which restored almost immediately the light of hope to her careworn face. She only asked one more question. She wanted to know what would become of her children in case she should die, and when I told her that children who once entered our Department of Education were always protected, clothed and supported, without the slightest dishonor, by the Association and afterward entered our Industrial Army on equal terms with all others, she seemed so happy that the bystanders wept and I felt my own eyes grow moist.

Several days after this, being anxious to learn the fate of this woman, whose name was recorded as Elizabeth Maxon, I entered, inquired at the office of the Domestic department, where she was enrolled, and learned that she had been assigned by her department chief to laundry work and that her place of residence was number 800 Pine Street. I took occasion to call there. Upon my ringing the electric bell the door was opened by a bright-faced little girl of about fifteen summers.

"Is your mother at home?" I asked.

"Yes," was the reply. "Will you come in?"

She ushered me through a small carpeted hallway, into a neatly furnished parlor, the floor of which was also carpeted, and the furniture in which appeared to be quite new. Having been politely offered a chair, I sat down, and being informed that "mamma" wold be in directly I waited. A minute later Mrs. Maxon appeared.

"Mrs. Maxon," I said, arising, "you will doubtless look upon my visit as an intrusion, but I felt so deep an interest in your welfare, after your application and examination for membership, that I had to hunt you up. Perhaps you will remember me as the man who presided at that time."

"Indeed!" she exclaimed. "Mr. Braden, certainly this is an honor and not an intrusion. You were so kind to me on that occasion that I shall never forget you. Will you be seated, sir?"

I sat down again. Mrs. Maxon also seated herself.

"I would be glad to learn how you fared," I resumed. "Will you permit me to ask you a few questions?"

"Yes, indeed!" was the quick answer. "I will answer any question. The people are so good to me here that I feel that you are all brothers and sisters. And see," (she waved her hand around her), "I have never lived in such a pleasant house before. It is heated by steam which comes from pipes laid under the streets and we have water, gas and electricity."

"Do you like your work?"

"It is very pleasant. Most of the work at the laundry is done by machinery and the machinery does five times as much work as the force we have there could do by hand. All the hard work is done by machinery. Then I have only to work seven hours a day, too."

"How did you get so well settled?"

"The next day after the examination I was told to go to the office of the Domestic department on Commonwealth Avenue. I went. The gentleman in charge told me that when an active member paid a membership fee of $100.00 the company gave a labor check to her in return representing $100.00 worth of goods. He gave me the amount in such check and then directed a gentleman to take me and my children to number 800 Pine Street, where we should live. He hailed a passing motor car and we got on that and rode to this house, my children with me. The gentleman did not pay my fare, but I paid it.

"I was surprised that it only amounted to what would be two cents of my hundred dollars. I was quite surprised also to find that we were to have such a nice house. But there was no furniture in it then. I left my children with our neighbor, and went up to the department house and ordered these carpets, furniture and other things. They let me have them on time, with the understanding that they were to keep the title until they were paid for. I got a few groceries from the store and some meat and brought them home myself. The furniture came about 2 o'clock that afternoon and before supper time we were almost settled. A bell rang out there in the dining room and I found a telephone there. I answered it and found that the foreman of the company which I was told to enter had some directions. He said I was to go over to the ward office of the Department of Education, about two blocks from here, and report with my children at 9 o'clock next morning and then to report to him at 9:30 o'clock for duty. So I did, and all my little ones were taken and sent to school."

"Are you then comfortable?"

"I am very, very happy. I never dreamed that such good would come to me after my husband died. But God has directed me here and I am very, very happy."

The conversation continued a few minutes longer. All her little children, with bright and shining faces, came in to see me, and I was overflowing with sympathetic enthusiasm myself before I was able to tear myself away. And I thought to myself as I returned to my home that the joy our system brought to these comparatively humble people was the best indication that we were now, in truth, upon the threshold of a higher civilization; a civilization that uses all power, both mechanical and human, to lift up all humanity; a civilization which does not content itself by simply emblazoning the golden rule upon painted banners and church walls, but makes it the measure of every public act toward all men, women and children alike.

CHAPTER XII.

IDAHO ELECTS A SENATOR—PARALYSIS OF THE COMPETITIVE SYSTEM—BLIGHT AFFECTS THE CAPITAL CITY—CAPITAL WITHDRAWS FROM THE STATE—A SESSION OF THE LEGISLATURE—CO-OPOLIS ESTABLISHES A DEPARTMENT STORE AND HOTEL AT BOISE CITY.

Governor Thompson was inaugurated at Boise City January, 1903. There was no demonstration on the occasion, the Governor being sworn in by the Chief Justice of the Supreme court of the state without display. The Legislature convened the same day, the Lower House elected its speaker, and the next day the various committees of both branches of the lawmaking body were appointed. The third day the entire political machinery of Idaho, with the exception of some minor officers and some members of the judiciary, was under the control of the Co-operators.

The work to be performed by the Legislature was regarded as pressing and important. A senator was to be elected to represent the state in the United States senate. The complexion of the two houses made it certain that the new senator would be a Co-operator. As for that matter so was the then incumbent. He was a member of the People's party and also a member of the Brotherhood and of the Co-opolitan colony. He was a man of wealth and, being past the age of forty-five, had transferred property to our colony worth twenty years of a Co-operator's income, estimated upon the basis of such income January 1st, 1902. In addition to this, his assistance as senator from Idaho had been invaluable to our cause. When a man became a member, in this manner, the Association, while leaving him his own property and the income which he derived from it, required that all wages, salaries and compensation, which his skill, labor or use of time might earn should be the property of the Association, so that the senator's yearly salary belonged to it. We took but one vote on the senatorial question, and the sitting senator was by that vote elected to succeed himself.

But this Legislature had some really serious questions to consider besides that of electing a senator. It was confronted by a condition which to all individuals in the state seemed appalling. The public, outside of the co-operative colonies in the state, and outside the Brotherhood of the Co-operative Commonwealth out of the state, was filled with alarm at the prospect of certain radical reforms being initiated.

The election of Governor Thompson and a co-operative Legislature was the signal for all banks, competitive business houses and money loaners to draw in their loans and investments, as far as possible, and many of those who were engaged in the various lines mentioned proposed to depart from the state. In such cities as Boise City, Shoshone, Ketchem and a few others of like description the saloon men and money loaners endeavored to sell out and leave the state at once.

The banks refused to make any new loans and insisted upon the immediate payment of such indebtedness as was then due. The railroad companies began a course of discrimination against the people of the state and business houses reduced their stocks of goods. Money, gold, silver and paper, became very scarce.

Boise City, the capital, before January 1st was in a condition of business paralysis. As for the several Co-operators, who made up the Legislature and occupied other government positions, they had no money—that is, United States gold, silver and paper. Their entire exchange consisted of the orders and checks already described. It was evident that they would not be able to pay cash for what they purchased in Boise and the merchants and other business men realized as early as December that they were not likely to reap a harvest from the new administration.

This was also anticipated by the Department of Commerce at Co-opolis, and an agent of the Legislative Council was sent down to Boise, who speedily closed a trade for a lot of land on Boise's principal street. Then came carloads of lumber from Co-opolis, and a force of Co-opolitan carpenters was speedily at work, even in the dead of winter, constructing a good, substantial and commodious three-story-high building. One-half of this building was a hotel and one-half a department store. By January 1st such was the energy displayed by the Co-opolitan workmen that it was completed and furnished and the store part was stocked with a large assortment of groceries, hardware, cutlery, drugs, clothing, dry goods, fancy goods, millinery, fruit, meats, boots and shoes, dairy products and many other of the manufactures and products of Co-opolis and the Co-opolitan farm.

This, to a very large extent, solved the problem of comfort and supplies for our representatives. The orders and checks of the Association were all good at the hotel and store. A few motorcycles with runners and others without and some horses and carriages were provided later on. The inferiority of the streets and roads in and around Boise at that time made horses indispensable in the conveyance of passengers in the winter time. The department stores undersold every other business and in a very short time its trade from the citizens and from the surrounding country was enormous. The competitive stores could not compete with them. The same was true of the hotel. The table creaked with the finest of Co-opolitan foods and delicacies prepared by the most expert of Co-opolitan cooks. The service at the hotel was excellent, the beds were clean and soft, and the attention given by our hotel attendants made up for the somewhat temporary character of the buildings.

Notwithstanding the complete prostration of town business and the absence of work for workmen, skilled and unskilled, the farmer and the cattle men around Boise began almost immediately to realize that it was an advantage to them. They obtained all manufactured goods at our department store cheaper than ever before. They were also able to exchange their products for department store wares.

The wheat, corn, oats and other staple products of the farm and cattle from the ranges still found as good a market abroad as ever and commanded as good prices. That was not saying very much, however, for prices everywhere ruled low.

State, municipal, county and other public bonds depreciated until their value was scarcely more than nominal. Miners and cattle men were nearly the only classes who were now able to pay taxes, and both classes were notoriously expert in evading this duty by false statements of their wealth. It was evident that before another year passed, if Idaho depended upon the money of the United States in circulation within her jurisdiction, for the payment of public expenses, that her condition was one of hopeless bankruptcy.

This condition did not much interest the rank and file of the Co-operators, because they were well satisfied with their labor-credit checks and industrial orders, which enabled them to obtain all they needed, even money, under certain restrictions. But the individualists were in despair and many of them emigrated with their flocks and herds to Wyoming. Others who considered that their holdings in Idaho were too valuable to leave, not understanding the Co-operators' plans, contented themselves with abusing what they called the stupidity of the administration. They knew it was the unalterable purpose of our people never to issue public bonds and this was the only method of raising money for public uses of which they had any knowledge. Some of them proposed the issuance of warrants upon the treasury, bearing interest after demand, but this was immediately rejected.

The proposition was made by one prominent individualist newspaper to issue treasury notes to circulate as money, but this was at once declared impracticable as being an encroachment upon the authority of the Federal government to coin money and the provision of the Federal constitution prohibiting the emission by the states of bills of credit. Turning then to state-bank issues the individualist found no encouragement from that quarter, as he was confronted by the Federal tax of ten per cent of such issues. Be it noted, however, that some of the bankers were inclined to favor the issue of state-bank notes and strongly advised that it be done, arguing that it was better to have money with the ten per cent tax rather than no money at all. But the administration simply declared that Co-operators did not feel the scarcity of money and a far better plan than any proposed would doubtless be discovered.

The Legislature remained in session just thirty days. Very few new laws were enacted. Of those which were enacted the reduction of all salaries of public officials one-half, the law providing for a constitutional convention, the delegates to which were to have no compensation except traveling expenses, the abolition of several offices, such as insurance commissioner, labor commissioner, etc., the repeal of the law authorizing corporations and the enactment of a law respecting the organization of Co-operative Associations and their regulation, were the most important. Some appropriations were made, but it was admitted to be one of the most economical sessions ever held by any legislative body, so far as results to the state were concerned. The law reducing salaries one-half, although not strictly applicable to existing officials, was effective because all Co-operators in office willingly complied with it, and that general compliance influenced individualists to do likewise.

CHAPTER XIII.

THE CONSTITUTIONAL CONVENTION AND ITS LABORS.

The constitutional convention was set for July 4th, 1903, at Co-opolis. The election was held two weeks before that time. Few individualists were anxious to become delegates because the honor was unaccompanied by compensation, and for the further reason the majority of Co-operators was now overwhelming. The result was that the same proportion of Co-operators obtained in the convention as in the Legislature and it was evident that the progress of the Co-operative Commonwealth would be carried out. When the convention met it was called to order by the Governor, a portion of whose address on that occasion is well worthy of repetition. After tracing briefly the history of Co-opolis and the Brotherhood of the Co-operative Commonwealth, in glowing language, he took up the question of the Co-operative Constitution and said:

"Gentlemen: You are the men in whose wisdom the state of Idaho confides and upon whose action here the fate of unknown generations hangs. I would not presume to advise you with regard to your all-important mission, but I shall ask permission to offer, with the greatest humility and with all respect for your high intelligence, a few simple suggestions.

"The burden of all I have to say can be aptly phrased in the somewhat homely language borrowed from the street. Do not put your state in a 'strait jacket.' Do not think it necessary to prohibit, restrict, define and dogmatize when you come to make your constitution.

"When you have provided a system of state government and made clean and emphatic the boundaries of executive, legislative and judicial power, consider that you have completed your work. Do not undertake to guard the inalienable rights **of man by** introducing details, methods **and** systems into your constitution. Leave all that to the common sense and common justice of the people. Let your **Legislature** dominate both the executive and judiciary. **That body is** designed, or should be, to express the popular **will.** The judiciary is designed to interpret that will as expressed. The executive is to carry that will into effect."

The Governor's address did not advance further into the province of the convention. He spoke, for the most part, in a merry **vein,** as if he felt that even if the success of his work was not yet achieved it had nearly passed the stage of experimentation, and when he concluded the convention, while impressed with the importance of its great mission, appeared to share in their leader's satisfaction.

The convention continued in session one week. The result of its work was a constitution, brief, clear and simple. It provided for executive and legislative departments. No judiciary was provided for. It prescribed the duties of the executive department and provided for its branches. The first Governor of Idaho was to hold office for a period of three years and all Governors succeeding for seven years each. He was the chief executive of the state and his duty was to see that the law was enforced.

There were to be a Secretary of State, State Auditor, State Treasurer, Attorney-General and Secretary of Co-operative Industries. The duties of these several officials were such as ordinarily attach to such officials, except that of Secretary of Co-operative Industries. It was the duty of this official to keep a full record of all Co-operative Associations in the state, their rules and by-laws, and to use his best endeavors to bring about a complete union of all under one head. He was also to be the active general of the militia of the state and superintend all operations of that body, subject to the order of the Governor. The Great Council possessed all legislative and judicial power. The legislative power could not be delegated, but was restricted and controlled by the people as follows: When twenty per cent of the voting population of the state should petition to have any law, whether on the statute books or not, submitted to popular vote, the Governor's duty was to submit it at the annual election held in October of each year. A majority vote was sufficient to enact or repeal such law.

It was also provided that if twenty per cent of the population should petition the President to remove any official from office the question of such removal should be submitted to the popular vote at the next annual election, and a majority vote was sufficient to retain or remove such official. In case such officer was removed by popular vote the Governor was to appoint a successor to hold until the next annual election, but the person removed could not hold the office again until one full term had intervened. The Legislature had power to delegate its judicial functions in such manner as it saw fit.

When it was desired to remove the Governor the petition must be submitted to the Great Council and in case of his removal the vacancy was filled by that body.

When the convention adjourned its labors had produced the briefest written constitution in force in any of the states of the American Union. In my opinion it was the best. It not only made the legislative body the most prominent of the people's servants, but it provided a plain and simple method for the exercise of such control. It provided a strong executive to execute the laws and made him the commander-in-chief of the militia of the state, both industrial and military, but it gave him no veto or pardoning power. It was, however, his province to recommend to the Great Council the pardon of persons sentenced by the judiciary to punishment, and few instances are known to our history where such recommendations were not acted upon favorably. It contained one brief provision which expresses all that is best in modern civilized government in a few words. That provision, under the head of Co-operation, is as follows:

"The Council shall provide for the government ownership of all the sources and machinery of production and the operation of the same, to the end that no person within the state shall be idle or needy. It shall cause all railroads, water rights, mines and cultivated or uncultivated lands to be purchased by the state as speedily as practicable and shall levy an army, to be known as the Industrial Army, to work the same. The state shall never sell, grant or alienate any of its property so acquired. No property shall be taken from any person or persons by the state without paying just compensation therefor."

All the laws in force at the time of the adoption of the new constitution, except such as were inconsistent with it, were to be continued in force until amended or repealed. All officials, except those whose offices were abolished by the new constitution, or should be abolished by the Great Council, continued in office until the next general election.

The constitutional election was held the third Monday in August, 1903, and resulted in the adoption of this new instrument. By its terms the old system of legislation being abolished, the Governor was authorized to convene the first session of the Great Council the first Monday in January, 1904. An election was called for November, and at that election the Great Council, consisting of one hundred and ninety members, representing as nearly as possible one for each one thousand voters, were elected. All but thirty were Co-operators. There was no doubt now that the new state and the new system were, for a time at least, established. The machinery of government was in our hands and the future rested with us.

The world beyond Idaho did not apparently concern itself with us or our system. The defeat of the opposition which had, in the election of 1902, attacked us with bitterness, resulted in that opposition subsiding into silence. The great dailies, magazines and periodicals simply refused to recognize us, and our system received no notice from the capitalist world. This was annoying to some of the Co-operators, both in and out of Idaho, because we felt that we were ignored and that our merits ought to be proclaimed. I remember some of our members of the Great

Council expressing dissatisfaction because of this fact in the presence of Governor Thompson.

"Merits!" exclaimed he; "what merits have we? We have simply shown the world that for five years we could work together and produce wonders. Let us see what we can do as lawmakers. Let us show what we can do with a state after we have captured it. If we make some blunders you need not flatter yourselves that you are unobserved. If you build a strong and substantial state you need not fear that the world will overlook that fact. The truth is that all the capital, intellect and classes of America are watching for signs of disagreement and dismembership. They will be disappointed if they do not find them, but when you are on a solid basis then they will proclaim your system a wonder and philosophers will come to observe and study it. We ought to bear all this in mind as we proceed to the work of making proper laws for the regulation of this state. Our history is just begun and it rests with us whether it will continue."

CHAPTER XIV.

DEPARTMENT STORES IN THE COMPETITIVE SYSTEM—DEPARTMENT STORES IN CO-OPERATION—THE CO-OPOLITAN ASSOCIATION DISCOVERS THE VALUE OF THE DEPARTMENT STORE AS A WEAPON OF WARFARE—THE DEATH OF OLD BOISE.

The latter part of the nineteenth century saw strange and novel influences at work in the competitive system of the civilized world. The great advantages accruing from co-operation had become apparent, in those days, to a few, and these employed its methods to a limited extent to acquire vast fortunes for themselves. Such were corporations, trusts, great combinations of capital, department stores and syndicates. These concerns, establishing themselves in every industrial center, absorbed nearly every industry. It was impossible for the individual, the small capitalist, the man, to compete with such institutions, and yet those who were the greatest gainers from them were the most zealous advocates of the competitive system. Wanamaker's vast department stores in Philadelphia and New York city were good illustrations of what the co-operative institution, employed against the co-operator, could accomplish, both for the one man who owned it and against the many who were asked to compete with it.

The owner grew fabulously rich. There was no limit to his acquisitions and he swallowed up all competitors who could not do business on the same system. Commercial house after commercial house fell before Wanamaker. Man after man became bankrupt, not because he lacked business ability, or was idle or inattentive, but because he could not compete with Wanamaker. So it came to pass that in Wanamaker's great marvels of industry, the department stores, some of the brightest, shrewdest and most expert business men were serving as managers of departments, floor walkers, clerks and bookkeepers. It was, indeed, a vast, ceaseless and mighty army of co-operators intent upon making the fortune of one man, and with such a combination competition could not compete.

In Idaho our colony accidentally discovered the use to which they could put this great "idea" which enabled Wanamaker to conquer the commercial world and force the princes of industry to become his willing slaves. This was the undesigned conquest of Boise City by the Co-operative Commonwealth. When the first Great Council met in January, 1904, our Co-operative Hotel had absorbed the entire business of all other hotels in the city.

All our productive power was so fully employed that we were able to furnish board and lodging for a small sum, of a quality such as few hotels in cities of a hundred thousand persons offered their guests. Our department store was equally successful.

It cost us nothing to advertise.

We painted no signs.

We paid no rents.

The only expense we incurred was the labor we expended, and labor was as plentiful as humanity.

Besides this, we employed labor-saving machinery without stint, and thereby multiplied the enormous power of co-operative labor many times.

We were better and more powerfully prepared to destroy competition than Wanamaker, because we had no expenses and wasted neither time nor money in inviting trade.

We sold daily the best wares and produce which we could manufacture or procure. The excellence of our stocks, together with the smallness of our prices, was our recommendation.

We intensified by our establishment in Boise City the well-known effects of the department store in competitive cities.

All the trade came to us.

Nothing could compete with our system, and merchants

and hotel men were compelled to assign for the benefit of creditors, join the Co-operative Commonwealth or depart from the state.

When our new constitution was adopted the Co-opolitan Legislative Council made a rule that all persons who were citizens of the state at that time should be eligible for membership on the same terms as all other members of the National Brotherhood. Most of the merchants and hotel men in Boise City whose occupations were gone chose to join our body and were assigned to positions in the Co-opolitan store or some suitable department at Co-opolis.

Lawyers being largely creatures of competition, nearly all disappeared, and the few who remained either joined us and were assigned to the Legal department or if they remained and did not join engaged in the precarious business of settling up bankrupt estates.

The Association had, with the opening of spring, purchased a pleasantly located tract of land adjoining the city, laid it out on the plan of Co-opolis as nearly as could be done, constructed elegant brick hotel and department store buildings, built a large number of cottages similar to those in Co-opolis, and a commodious school building, and provided water, gas, electric and steam-heating plants. About November 1st, 1903, the entire Co-opolitan plant in Boise City, including the industrial force employed, removed to the new town and old Boise was well nigh deserted.

The reason for this move is apparent.

Old Boise was burdened by debt which it was no part of the design or duty of the Co-operative Commonwealth or of the Co-opolitan colony to pay.

There was a large bonded municipal debt, a large bonded water debt and another large school debt.

The gas and electric plants were also bonded, but those were private debts payable only by such as availed themselves of their advantages.

There was no way to avoid assuming these public debts if we continued in the old city.

Some of our enemies, later on, set up a howl against what

they termed our immorality in running away from these obligations. But they were not our obligations. We did not make them and we certainly had a right to live outside of the territory affected by them if we chose. In competitive cities business enterprises and persons of integrity and fortune usually locate where the public burdens are least likely to rest heavily upon them.

While Boise City, that is the collection of town lots, streets and buildings bearing that historic designation, was blighted, the collection of people who had done all the work of building it was immeasurably improved by the Co-operative accession. A new Boise City had begun to grow up on the commercial ruins of the old, but the Boston, New York, St. Louis and Chicago people who held large tracts of land around about and in the city were not benefited by this change. New Boise did not help them. Indeed, their land depreciated in price daily.

The banks of old Boise all went into liquidation and made frantic efforts to collect their debts.

Money loaners did the same.

Insurance agents either fled from the blight or came to us.

Saloonkeepers, speculators in land, dance-hall proprietors, persons whose methods of gaining a livelihood were illegal, women of ill reputation and gamblers all departed for lands unknown.

From the competitive point of view this hegira was regarded as a fatal blow to old Boise. Useless as were their occupations to the production or even distribution of wealth, they had been deemed necessary, because they lured money into the city, and this money, being collected in fines from one class and taxes from another class, went to help pay interest on public bonds. Many a pious holder of municipal bonds would be shocked to learn that but for the toleration of criminal and disgusting practices in the bonded city the bond would be well nigh worthless. Yet such was the case.

The Legislative Council of the city of Co-opolis took full

notice of the situation at Boise and after visiting and viewing the city felt and expressed great pleasure. It was our first venture into a competitive city, and at the outset we had entertained some misgivings as to the probabilities of a success. But the seeming necessity of providing accommodations for a Co-operative Legislature forced us to enter Boise City and the results were astonishing. The profits were immense, and it was now evident that the co-operative system was not only a powerful developer of a new and hitherto unoccupied country, but that in very truth it was invincible in the very center of competition. Honesty, justice and fraternity, in combination with industry, were unconquerable, and left no room for the gambler, the speculator, the panderer or the drone. This discovery having been made, the Legislative Council announced its purpose to place a department store and hotel in every city in the state, but to proceed cautiously, so as not to diminish the annual dividends of members.

By the employment of this great industrial force it was believed the citizens of Idaho would speedily be brought to enlist in and share the benefits of the Co-operative Commonwealth. And events have proved the belief correct.

CHAPTER XV.

OUR NEW REVENUE SYSTEM—CONSTITUTIONAL BATTLE OVER BILLS OF CREDIT—MONEY IN IDAHO—CONFLICTS WITH CATTLE MEN AND MINE OWNERS—CO-OPERATION AGAINST THE FIELD.

The Great Council of 1904 readjusted our legal system to conform to the new constitution and the co-operative programme. The political subdivision of the state into counties was not disturbed and local government of these was delegated to county commissioners. What had been variously denominated home rule and local option was, however, greatly extended.

Counties were permitted to determine for themselves many questions which by the old system were within the exclusive province of the Legislature. No county or other subdivision of the state was permitted to issue bonds for any purpose nor to expend in any one year more than the total amount received in taxes. But each county had the option to pay the state tax in money or in the products of labor. Where a county voted to pay taxes in the products of labor it was required to maintain as many store houses as were necessary to properly and securely store its receipts.

The law provided that the Great Council should annually elect a commission consisting of five members, whose duty it was to meet at the capital city in October of each year and determine the value of the various products of the state. The cereals, for instance, were to be valued at so much per bushel, vegetables and fruit at so much per pound, precious metals at so much per ounce, wool, hides, furs and other raw material at such prices as were fixed in the schedule prepared by the commission. All articles named in the schedule were to be received in lieu of money and at the prices fixed, so long as that schedule remained in force.

This plan would have been impracticable had it not been for the fact that the Legislative Council of Co-opolis agreed to take all produce so received for taxes at the schedule price therefor. The latter, for its own protection, placed a department store in every county seat, where, under its contract, it reserved all perishable property and either sold it in the proper department of its local store or shipped it at once to a suitable market. The schedule prices were sufficiently low to protect the Co-opolitan Association from loss. As for hides, furs, wool and other raw material, and staple agricultural products, they were carefully inspected by Co-opolitan commissioners at the receiving department store or warehouse, and, if not of schedule standard, were not accepted. In this manner and by this system all producers were able to pay their taxes without being compelled to borrow money and in the very wealth which their industry produced.

All public expenses were defrayed and all salaries were paid in the products of labor. The salary of a judge, for instance, amounting to twelve hundred dollars per annum, neither more nor less than a Co-opolitan received as his annual dividend, was paid by the state in orders or credit checks for goods or whatever the Co-opolitan Association had to sell. Such orders were of various denominations and in the following form:

To the Co-opolitan Association:

Deliver to the bearer hereof goods, wares, merchandise, entertainment or services of the value of one dollar and charge the same to the State of Idaho.

  Jacob Wirth,   John Thompson,
    Secretary.   Governor.

This method of collecting taxes and paying state expenses proved fully equal to the emergency. The Co-opolitan Association lost nothing by it. All schedule prices were fixed, as I have already stated, at a figure which was slightly lower than the cash market price for non-perish-

THE CO-OPOLITAN. 95

able and staple products and still lower for produce generally considered perishable.

But the producer also found his advantage to consist in the facility with which it enabled him to meet his public dues at all times promptly, thus avoiding penalties, interest and expenses. The system had not been long in operation before a question arose, concerning these orders, with the Federal authorities, who, at first, pronounced the Co-opolitan Association a kind of a banking institution, and the state orders upon it devices in the nature of state bank issues. The effort was then made to compel the Co-opolitan Association to pay the ten per cent tax imposed by the Federal law on such issues.

The question was never brought into the courts, because the most eminent and expert lawyers in the Union agreed that such orders could no more be regarded as money than the checks of business men upon their bank deposits, the promissory notes of debtors, the tickets of transportation companies and the time checks of mining and other large corporations controlling labor.

Another question arose of a more serious character upon the right of the state to emit "Bills of Credit." This the Federal constitution prohibited. A test case was made upon one of the state orders and taken to the United States Supreme Court. The decision of that tribunal was rendered by a divided court, a majority being of opinion that they could not be regarded as coming within the prohibition of the constitution referred to. These orders, the court held, were not designed to circulate as money, because they were directed to a private association of individuals designated as the Co-opolitan Association, and simply directed such association to deliver goods to the bearer. It was not a promise on the part of the state to pay money, nor to deliver goods. It was to be honored on demand, and when received by the Association in question was forthwith canceled. Evidence was offered by the parties seeking to void the orders that as a matter of fact they did circulate as money. This was held to be immaterial, for the reason that the fact, if shown, would not tend to prove that such was the intention of the state. The truth was that very few of the state orders so circulated. They were usually presented to the Co-opolitan store at any county seat without intermediate transfer, and a labor-credit check or industrial orders were issued instead.

It is true that such industrial orders so circulated and were treated as money by the people of Idaho, but the practice was not encouraged by Co-operators, because it was an incident of individualism and not of co-operation. Their circulation could not be prevented so long as the co-operative plan embraced the purchase of all property owned or produced by individualists in the state, and payment on goods or property as represented by these orders. In 1904 more than one-half of the people of the state were members of the Co-opolitan Association, and great numbers of those who were not members were daily becoming so. It was believed that in time our industrial orders would cease to circulate and perhaps be entirely superseded by the labor-credit check. It should be borne in mind that the labor-credit check, not being transferable, never passed out of the hands of its owner.

The policy of Idaho and the Co-opolitan Association was to prevent, as far as possible, the circulation of money in the state. It was treated as if it were a kind of poison which produced among men most dreadful diseases, and at the same time was an instrument of moral, financial and social ruin. We were fully convinced, when Co-opolis was founded, that if co-operation was to succeed some system must be applied which would exclude money from use among Co-operators. But it was recognized that outside of Idaho money was and must continue to remain king, as long as the industrial competitive and individualist system governed their affairs. For this reason the Co-opolitan Legislative Council accepted money, but sought in every possible way to prevent its circulation.

All money obtained by the sale of surplus products, manufactures or property of any kind in other states, or which might come into the co-operative stores, was immediately turned over to the Legislative Council and by it deposited in a strong safe in the basement of the Council Hall. Here it was guarded as if it were a deadly peril to the public weal.

The safe in which it rested was opened by a combination known only to the President, and it stood in an iron chamber whose great lock was turned by a key held by one of the Council. This was enclosed in another iron chamber which was opened only by a different key held by another member of the Council. There were twenty-six chambers of different sizes, the smaller enclosed within the larger, and twenty-six locks opened by as many different keys, each councilor holding one and no more. It took twenty-six councilors and twenty-six keys to reach the safe, and no money could be taken from it except in the presence of at least one-half of the members of the Legislative Council. But it was a rule of the Association that if any person living in the state desired money with which to travel outside of the state he should make his affidavit to that effect setting forth the amount he desired, and upon his application for such an amount, if the Council were satisfied that it was made in good faith and that the money would not be expended in the state, the application was granted. Articles which the Department of Commerce were compelled to import from other states or countries were also paid for from the accumulation in the safe.

After disposing of the question of how taxes and public expenses could be discharged the first Great Council took up the question of what property should be taxable. Among the private individualist enterprises in Idaho mining and grazing predominated. Both the mine owners and cattle men, whose herds were permitted to wander at will on the ranges, were expert "tax dodgers." How to reach them and compel them to pay their just and fair proportion of the expense of running the state and maintaining the schools was an important question. It was decided that all taxes should be levied on land values. In other words, what is sometimes called the Single-Tax system was adopted.

Wherever cattle men occupied a range together the total number of cattle upon it was determined, owners' names were obtained and the value of the range per acre was estimated upon the basis of its use for grazing purposes. Each owner was then made liable for the tax on the total acreage of the range occupied, and the proportion each was bound to pay was no question for the state, but was a question for the cattle men to determine for and among themselves. Cattle men now found it impossible to escape their taxes as formerly, each being zealous to require his neighbor to pay his part, and it must be confessed that they showed a strong disposition to leave the state, so that the ranges abandoned by them were left for the use of our herds.

It ought to be said, however, that the cattle owners did not abandon the state without a fight. They resisted the collection of taxes, claiming the system to be unjust and against public policy. One of the trial courts decided in their favor, but the case was appealed to the Great Council, which, it will be remembered, retained the Supreme Judicial authority in itself. The matter was referred by this body to six of its members, all lawyers, and indeed the only lawyers in the Great Council, all of whom were Co-operators, and the trial court was reversed. There was also an armed resistance to the collection of the tax, but the cattle men were speedily put to rout, the state militia suffering no other loss than three men wounded. The newspaper press throughout the Union, however, took sides with the cattle men, claiming that the system of taxation had been adopted for the sole purpose of driving these "honest" men from the state and taking possession of "their" ranges. The truth was that the men who left the state on account of this law did so to escape honest burdens and went where the laws were more unjust, or if not unjust not effectual to prevent the shifting of such burdens dishonestly to other shoulders which ought not to bear them. We offered no encouragement to dishonest practices, and if our failure to do so was an advantage to some other state which did we certainly had no occasion to feel envious.

Mining property owned by corporations or associations was valued at the full par of its capital stock and assessed accordingly.

It was the policy of the state not to encourage the mining of the precious minerals by private enterprise. The miners of the state were fast becoming absorbed in our Co-opolitan Association and wages had risen to nearly four dollars per day for skilled or unskilled workers, because a membership in the Co-opolitan Association or its Industrial Army paid that amount annually.

Mine owners sought to obviate what they called the evil of high wages by importing cheaper labor. At first they attempted the introduction of Chinese miners and later an ignorant class of Italians, Hungarians and Slavonians. Our Great Council prohibited aliens from owning, holding or acquiring real estate or making investments of any kind within the state on and after the date of the passage of a law to that effect. It also prohibited the importation of aliens into the state as laborers, or the employment of any such by any person, association or corporation.

These laws were all held to be valid and constitutional by the Supreme Court of the United States, which some years after their passage had occasion to pass upon them.

The result was that capital engaged in mining in Idaho withdrew and some of the mines were purchased at a low figure and operated by the Co-opolitan Association.

Here again the press of the United States denounced the immorality of the Co-operative Commonwealth, because of its oppressive conduct toward capital. Immoral indeed!

Idaho simply made laws which in other states or countries have never been disapproved as immoral.

The Co-opolitan Association gave to labor the same high wages in all its departments, and in that manner made laborers anxious to join the Association. This left the mine owner to do his own work or pay as much as the worker could earn as a Co-operator.

The capitalist could not compete in the labor market with labor itself, when labor employed its skill and force in its own behalf. If the mine which was made to produce wealth for capital and peril, distress and death for labor, became valueless, because there was no longer a force to work it, whose fault was that?

We did not steal the gold which glistened in its dark caverns!

We did not rob the capitalist of the labor which he owned!

The labor of men and women was not his vested right, like his mine. He had preached the merits of competition and we had simply competed for and won the labor force that dug his mine.

Now the mine was worthless because the men who made it would no longer work it. What did the Co-opolitan Association do which was immoral? Having taken its labor force and set it at work for itself, this mine had no value except if the labor force could be restored to it.

Capital could not do it. The Co-opolitan Association could. We purchased it for what it was worth without the labor force, which nobody owned. We could never have done this if capital had been able to work that same force and steal its products. Yet the newspaper press of that day denounced us as immoral and was effusive in its praise of the competitive system.

The Great Council at this session provided for a Supreme Judicial Court and as many County Courts as there were counties. The purpose of this system was to secure the proper administration of justice.

The Supreme Court was not authorized to decide any question of the constitutionality of a law enacted by the Great Council adversely, but if in their opinion such law was unconstitutional they were required to certify the same, with their reasons, to the Great Council for review. The jury system was preserved, with the exception that in civil cases a majority of the jury decided. Many radical changes were effected by this Great **Council, but those** mentioned **were** the most sweeping.

The Great Council of 1904, **perhaps because it was un**handicapped by precedents, **was the most memorable, for the** swiftness and **merit** of its **legislative work, of any session** which has occurred **since. Its successors had been, in a very** marked degree, **required by public sentiment to conform to its** standards.

Humanity, as all history proves, when once it accepts a system, whether good or bad, is loath to abandon it, and permits it to be changed only when the necessity for change is made apparent by experiences often of the most distressing nature. For this reason revolution has rarely **ever** produced lasting results except **in the mere form, and** not in the substance and **spirit** of things. If it be contended that society has undergone great changes in those respects let it be remembered that evolution, not revolution, did it.

CHAPTER XVI.

MISS CAROLINE WOODBERRY AGAIN—THE WEST PARISH—PUBLICATION OF MISS WOODBERRY'S NOVEL—MARRIAGE—WE VISIT NEW ENGLAND.

Long before the year 1904 drew to its close a great change had taken place in my life. The feminine disposition of my aunt to make matrimonial matches had been successful in throwing me into the society of Miss Caroline Woodberry and after the ride to Canyon Lake, of which I have already made mention, I was with her whenever leisure and opportunity permitted.

In Co-opolis there were in all seasons amusements and entertainments of every kind, and if we tired of one we were not at a loss for diversion which, while it could not increase the happiness I found in the young lady's society, aided me in administering to her pleasure. Society in Co-opolis was even then refined and intelligent. I do not mean to leave the impression that our people had in six years acquired all the arts and foibles which fashionable society in eastern cities mistake for refinement, but it really was wonderful to see what improvement prosperity had produced in the manner, bearing and language of most of our people. While it is possible that such prosperity in the competitive system, would have caused many to develop the worst traits of their character, yet the absence of all opportunity to amass a fortune in speculation or by gambling methods in the co-operative system insured to each the enjoyment of his own portion. Nobody was or could be purse proud. Nobody was or could be dependent upon charity. Nobody had occasion to be ashamed of his material condition.

Good clothes, ornaments, books, pleasant homes and all the conveniences of modern life were within the reach of all.

Humanity is so constituted, however, that its members must compete, contend and battle with one another.

What shall be the field for this competition? Over what shall the race contend? Where shall be the battle ground?

Some philosophers in times past taught that the race must fall into decay, dwindle into weakness and lose individuality if it was removed from the struggle for potatoes, meat and coffee. They, perhaps, honestly believed that it was fatal to progress to raise mankind to an elevated plane and let the battle be waged for moral, intellectual and perhaps spiritual supremacy. In Co-opolis our system eliminated the mere material world as an object of competition, and pursuing the law of our nature, we sought to excel in intellectual pursuits, matters of taste, athletics and what tended to personal improvement. It was not long before the Co-opolitan began to be known as being possessed of good manners, taste in matters of dress and even polish. These were not pronounced characteristics for many years after, but I sometimes thought I could see them developing. One manners, taste in matters of dress and even polish. These people from whom, in part, at least, the incentive to acquire and own things had been largely removed, lost in a measure the cheating, lying, cunning and overreaching habits of that delusive and obstructing thing called business. Co-opolitans, six years after the city was founded, habitually told one another the truth.

Sets and circles existed then, as now, in Co-opolitan society. Men and women always will choose their own companions and some common interest will always operate to form them into associations. If some of the potato diggers discover that potato digging is not all there is of life those will probably come to recognize in one another kindred spirits whose kinship is closer than that of the uninitiated and the circle is evolved. I was one of a circle or set and Miss Woodberry was a member of that circle, too. There were literary gatherings, card parties, socials and all sorts of meetings in winter, and lawn parties, dinners, dances and all sorts of pleasures in summer. It must be admitted that our social circle was generally regarded as somewhat select in a literary sense, because some of the brightest minds in Co-opolis were members. This did not exclude us from the pleasures which I have mentioned, but it gave our circle a somewhat sombre rather than gay reputation. We were just as popular, however, as any other set, and by no means assumed to be better than our neighbors.

 Miss Woodberry was not a member of the Industrial Army, and one of the great questions which we often discussed was whether she should become such. This question grew more than ever urgent when we decided that we were sufficiently attached to each other to become husband and wife. Attached to each other! That sounds and reads mechanical enough to describe the gluing together of two blocks of wood, and I have no doubt that because this is, in the main, an historical work and only incidentally biographical, it is all the warmth I am expected to express. I beg pardon! But this lady has been my wife now thirty years and a better wife no mortal man ever had. Attached to her! Why! I was so thoroughly and passionately devoted to her that I came very near incurring the censure of my department associates and being subjected to the operation of the Imperative Mandate on the charge of inattention to business, but escaped, because, as I suppose, "the whole world loves a lover," and my attachment was not successfully concealed. Be that as it may, after we were engaged to be married, Miss Woodberry became curious to know what her fate would be; she had accepted me without much regard to consequences. Now, after the acceptance, when the consequences were close at hand, she became more solicitous to understand her position. She had only been a visitor in Co-opolis and had been a guest of the Prestons, whom I have already described as my near neighbors. During this visit she had been engaged in writing a novel, which she read as the chapters were completed to me. I was impressed with its merit and believed some of its passages breathed the spirit of genius. However, although I judged myself a dispassionate and unsparing critic, I would not trust my judgment upon the production of one who was prejudiced in her favor. I persuaded her to allow me to submit her manuscript to a committee of my department for its criticism, with a view to arranging for its publication under the auspices of the Co-opolitan Association. As this committee had proven whenever it deemed a work sufficiently meritorious to warrant it, to proceed with its publication and defray the expenses from the so-called publication fund, it occurred to me that, if my judgment should be approved, this novel could be published by our department and would distinguish the admission of its author into the Association. We had, up to that time, never undertaken the publication of a novel, but our plant was sufficiently extensive and commodious to enable us to do so. Hitherto we were contented to confine our publications to text books for our schools, a monthly magazine devoted to co-operation, the Daily Co-opolitan and a large number of pamphlets. To my great joy the committee, composed of the very brightest literary men in the city, including our educational chief, Mr. Edmunds, pronounced it a production of such merit as to be worthy of publication at the public expense. I had not disclosed to them the name of the author and they supposed it was some member.

On the evening of the day when this decision was communicated to me I went over to the Preston cottage to see my affianced and tell her the result of my venture with the committee. She was delighted with the news. It was her first novel, and to find that the committee had received it with favor was an event which, as she often told me, gave her more genuine pleasure than anything ever did before or has since. We spent an hour or more that evening talking over the novel, its characters and plot.

The name was "The West Parish." The opening scene was laid in the West Parish of Gloucester, Cape Ann, Essex County, Massachusetts. There were, as everybody knows, wonderful descriptions of white sandy beaches, the blue old ocean, ships sailing, marshes and sea birds a-wing. There were two little boys and an old aunt. The former were orphans, the latter infirm and impoverished, but doing her best, which was as bad as could be, to keep the little ones alive. Their father had been a railroad engineer, but a series of misfortunes deprived him of his savings, and then, in one of the perils common to his dangerous employment, he was killed and the mother soon after died.

These little ones, without means and without the sympathy of the multitudes, who, in their desperation in the struggle for bread, forgot or did not see them, were sent to this aunt. That poor old woman had griefs enough of her own. Her life was well nigh worked out. She had neither nerves nor strength. Her limbs were stiff and rheumatic. Her eyes were dim and her aged back was bent. In her mean little cottage by the roadside at Annisquan she had all she could do to nurse the fading embers of her life's fires, and she was now expected to support these two little infants, one three and one five years of age. She was cross to them, but she did not mean to be. She was very impatient and she did not know it. She did not take them into her arms as a mother would, but that never occurred to her. And yet she loved them, but the power of expressing love had long been crushed out by poverty.

So one day these two ragged, half-fed little boys, with their tear-bestained cheeks and great eyes, made more expressive by being set in the pale faces pinched by want, started out from the old aunt's house in search of a place their mother used to tell them about which was called Heaven, where she said their papa was. The children were afterward found nearly starved to death lying near the roadside seven miles from home by some charitably disposed persons, who fed them and subsequently caused them to be placed in an orphan asylum, where they were kept and given a meagre education suitable to their lowly financial condition. When they were large and strong enough they were sent to the West and placed in the charge of farmers, but were widely separated. The author traced the development of each. Both were naturally possessed of powerful minds. One became a money maker, the other the champion of a new system for the development of **his** race. One was a great banker and amassed millions. **The** other was a great co-operator and occupied a high station in the Co-operative Commonwealth. She carried her story into the future that she might picture conditions which had not yet obtained.

In those days it was a favorite method of illustrating economic principles, and had been made quite fashionable by Bellamy's famous work called "Looking Backward." Miss Woodberry's novel was not so remarkable for its plot as for the vivid contrast which it presented between the competitive and co-operative system, and so powerfully did her pen draw the picture that while the brother who gave his life to the one, though not worse than most of its supporters, seemed possessed of a demon of greed; the brother who gave his life to the other appeared to be no more **nor** less than a man. This novel seemed to me then, as it **does** now, both instructive and artistic and equal to any of those which my wife has written since.

"What shall we do now?" asked Miss Woodberry. "You **have** obtained a favorable criticism and the Association will publish the novel. What advantage will it give me or you to do so?"

"I shall urge you first to make an application for membership," I replied. "Although you were not a citizen of Idaho nor a member of the National Brotherhood, you will find that your accomplishments and this novel will gain you immediate admission."

"Yes!" exclaimed she. "But what else? Does not **the** Co-opolitan Association provide for some reward for **a** meritorious work?"

"The Co-opolitan Association will endeavor to be just," I replied. "In the **case** of Dupont, the man who invented the Dupont motorcycle, which **has** brought us a large accession of wealth, the Legislative Council has allowed him a five years' furlough and he is now traveling in Europe, but draws his full pay on the Industrial Army. Dupont has decided to take only one year now and then the rest of his time hereafter. Then there is Dr. James, who received a furlough of three months and an advance of $1,200.00 from his next three years' pay, for special merit and extraordinary services of a professional character. We have a system of rewarding those who display special merit or who by some new invention add to the wealth, comfort or power of the Association.

"Our Legislative Council requests each department chief to present, every three months, the names of members most deserving of reward, and after fully and fairly informing themselves as to the work, art or production recommended, dispenses its rewards according to its best judgment. At the last meeting of the Legislative Council for this purpose ten men in my department were rewarded. One got six weeks rest, another two months, a third one week and others various terms of respite. This was in addition to the vacation. I am not in the habit of selecting these ten myself. I leave that to my foreman and in doing so avoid jealousies. I shall not recommend you, but I believe this novel will suggest to the Legislative Council the propriety of a reward."

This reference to her entering some department suggested the old discussion again of whether she would apply or not. She was very much attached to the Association and believed it would ultimately own the entire state, but she was not sure, she said, that she ought to become absorbed in it. We considered that we might marry and that I could supply the house from my income and she could, if her novel was successful from a financial point of view, do other literary work at home and for ourselves. But she was not committed to this view, nor were her opinions fixed. However, she finally agreed with me in the belief that her life could be made far more useful as a member than as an individual. We agreed that if both were employed by the Association our united efforts would bring us twenty-four hundred dollars a year so long as twelve hundred dollars was each member's income. I had long before converted all the property which I had inherited into cash of the gold and silver kind and had turned it over to the Association with the understanding that I would be permitted to withdraw it in amounts not greater than $1,200.00 per annum, if I so desired. The Association paid nothing for its use, but agreed to furnish, on the terms stated, goods, wares, labor checks or orders instead of money, or even money, if the proper affidavit and application for money was filed.

Aunt Lydia had also been economical in expenditures for the house, so that my expenses for two years had only been two thousand dollars, and I had a thousand dollars in unexpended labor-credit checks. This was also left with the Association, undrawn, so that the Association was indebted to me in the sum of $11,000.00. My affianced wife, as well as myself, was anxious to visit Europe and Asia, and this fund of $11,000.00 we calculated would enable us to do so without pinching ourselves while abroad. It was not possible to pinch ourselves at home, because at this time every department was accomplishing wonders in the production of wealth.

Caroline made her application the next day. Being neither a citizen of Idaho nor a member of the Brotherhood, she was obliged to pass an examination as to health, opinions and wealth. The first was found to be perfect. The second showed her to be fully acquainted with co-operative principles and the main features of our peculiar system. Wealth she had none. But she had what was better than wealth. She had talent. She had education. She had some experience in teaching and was a skillful stenographer. She was accepted and enrolled in the Educational department. This was in June and her services were not required until September in that department. She was, however, placed on the pay roll and given her vacation period at once. It did not concern the department whether her school year began or closed with a season of rest. I, too, was entitled to a vacation of four weeks each year, and it was usual for me to take it in July or August. Ordinarily I spent it in the vicinity of the great lakes in the northern part of the state or with parties of excursionists in the mountains. This year I designed to visit New England and to take with me my wife. Caroline was agreeable to this plan and I made all arrangements accordingly.

In the latter part of June we were married and on the very same day, as a part of the celebration, the work of putting the new novel into type was begun. It was a joyful occasion. The wedding ceremony was performed at my house in Co-opolis and Governor Thompson did me the honor to officiate. It was not a public affair. Members of the Legislative Council, Governor Thompson and the members of my departmental staff and their wives were present at the wedding feast, which was spread at the Co-opolitan Hotel. That evening my wife and I took a special car at 11:30 o'clock on the Co-opolis Southern Electric Railroad for Boise City, from which place we went to Nampa, met the early morning east-bound train on the Union Pacific and proceeded on our wedding trip.

We were absent until the middle of August and were glad enough to return. I say we were glad to return, but this does not mean that our trip was unpleasant. We were like people of refinement who gayly abandon the luxurious surroundings of a beautiful Christian home and, returning to the primitive habits of their savage ancestry, descend, for a short season, to the novelty of camp life. However enjoyable such life may seem for a season there comes a time, and that speedily, when the novelty wears off, and life in the civilized world is all the more pleasurable by comparison. So you descend into the regions of commercial competition, the waste regions and desert lands of speculation; the world where old men and women are left to die in poverty after a life of usefulness; where little children, innocent of wrong, are trained daily to sin, or are starved to death in sight of plenty. We were glad to return to Co-opolis and take up our labors in a land where we could not hope to acquire more of the world's good than we could use, but where we could be sure that we and ours would not be compelled to try subsistence on less than we needed, and where every human being was guaranteed "the inalienable rights of life, liberty and the pursuit of happiness."

CHAPTER XVII.

THE UNITED STATES CONVEYS PUBLIC LAND TO THE STATES—THE CO-OPOLITAN ASSOCIATION RECLAIMS THE SNAKE RIVER VALLEY—A GREAT AND BENEFICENT ENTERPRISE.

The year 1905 witnessed the inauguration of two important enterprises in Idaho, each of which has contributed immeasurably to the development of the Co-operative Commonwealth. Both were proposed, superintended and owned by the Co-opolitan Association. The first was the irrigation, cultivation and settlement of the Snake River Valley. This valley at that time was noted for its wonderful scenery, its broad expanse of uncultivated and unoccupied land, and the majestic river which swept swiftly through it. All public lands belonging to the United States had, the year before, been granted to the various states in which they were situated, each state being required to pay two cents an acre to the Federal government therefor. Some of the states proceeded to pay at once and receive the patent for the lands so granted, and to dispose of the same to settlers.

Among those which paid for their acquisitions promptly was Idaho. But the money to pay, amounting to one million three hundred and eighty-six thousand dollars, was advanced to Idaho by the Co-opolitan Association. This advance, let it be understood, was not a loan. The state government could not borrow money. But the Co-opolitan Association had become so powerful and exercised such entire and absolute control over the state government that when it advanced this amount it was well understood that it was able to reimburse itself at will. The state now acquired the public lands of the Federal government, but was powerless to improve them. What should be done?

The Great Council had met during the first half of the year, and its members were all Co-opolitans except eleven. It realized that it would be open to severe criticism outside of the state if it should grant the newly acquired lands to the Co-opolitan Association, whether for a consideration or gratuitously. It did not concern Idaho what the world beyond its territory thought, except that we were all anxious that mankind, for its own good, should not be misled as to the benefits of co-operation. Before that session of the Great Council was closed a petition, signed by more than twenty per cent of the voters of the state, was submitted to the Governor, on the recommendation of the Great Council itself, asking that the simple question of whether the public lands of the state should be granted in fee simple absolute to the Co-opolitan Association on condition that the Association improve the same, be submitted to popular vote at the October election. Under our law it was the duty of the Governor, if such petition was properly signed, to submit the question proposed as a matter of course, and it was done accordingly.

This was not the first time the people had by petition initiated legislation, but it was the most important question thus far submitted. There was no doubt as to the result, because the Co-opolitan Association embraced nearly all the people of the state except something like fifty thousand who were scattered along the boundaries of Montana and Wyoming, being principally placer miners and cattle men. Even among these there were many inclined to favor the grant. But the question was very fully discussed. The Daily Co-opolitan, under my charge, presented the arguments on all sides. Every company in the Industrial Army was required to attend at least three meetings before election day, at which the question was debated by the ablest debaters we could find, and on election day it is safe to say that the voters who were ignorant of the merits of this question were exceedingly few. The election resulted in a vote of two hundred and sixteen thousand five hundred and three for and seven thousand three hundred and twenty

THE CO-OPOLITAN. 113

against the grant. The decision of the people thus registered was the law of the state and was sufficient in itself to pass the title in all this land to the Association, but the formality of issuing the patent was enacted when the Great Council met the following January.

Great were the preparations the day after election for the work of reclaiming the Snake River Valley. The Legislative Council was in constant session arranging the details of an industrial occupation of a new and broader domain. The Engineering department had long before procured complete surveys of all the public lands, and more especially of this valley. A final survey had been made for an extensive system of irrigation flumes, canals and ditches, together with reservoirs for the collection and storage of surface waters, as well as the waters diverted from the river. Four thousand men were dispatched, under the charge of the proper departments, to commence the work and make excavations along the survey at such points as they could work most conveniently, and when the freezing of the ground in the latter part of November made further work in that direction impracticable the army returned to Co-opolis and the companies composing it were sent to their several home cities and engaged in other employment.

When springtime came—the spring of 1906—the work upon the irrigating system of Snake River Valley was again resumed with an increased force. It was prosecuted with such vigor that when the snow began to fly again the whole system was completed and constituted the most extensive of the kind on the American continent. The result was that one million acres of land as fertile as any in the world, not excepting the valley of the Nile, were made available for use for agricultural purposes and all of this was the property of the Co-opolitan Association. The whole of this broad area was now turned over to the Agricultural department. The Transportation department was also instructed to extend the Co-opolis Southern Electric Railroad the entire length of the valley, and in two years from the time the first work was done on the irrigating system that marvelous region was changed from a wilderness into a productive and beautiful garden.

The history of the Snake River region since then has been one of the most startling illustrations of the power of co-operation and the quantity of literature devoted to the description of the valley, its people, its productivity, its cities, roads, system and methods in all the countries and languages of the civilized world show how deep an impression this magnificent product of co-operation has made. But the wealth which this valley added each year to the Co-opolitan Association enabled us to carry the industrial war forward with a celerity not anticipated. The Agricultural department now—1909—had under its control three million five hundred thousand acres of land devoted to agriculture, five hundred thousand acres devoted to fruit and at least eight million devoted to grazing.

The Co-opolitan Association was and is the most successful farmer in the world! **No wonder!** There stand between it and the consumer **no middleman and no** manufacturer. Its own labor manufactures most of its own farm tools and machinery. It feeds, clothes and shelters its own farm hands, and both produces and manufactures food and clothing. All represent to it the cost of labor only. The wheat produced cost the Association in 1909 only about five cents per bushel to produce. This estimate is based upon the cost of machinery imported from other states and paid for with metallic money. But even this was too high an estimate, because when a machine was once imported our mechanics kept it in constant repair, while other farmers using machinery are continually paying out money to keep it in serviceable condition.

We paid nothing but labor. Other farmers were compelled to sell their wheat at the lowest cash price paid by traders and speculators, who invariably received a large profit. We obtained that profit ourselves. Other farmers saw their wheat ground into flour and sold at a profit by the manufacturer to the wholesale dealer, who again sold at a profit to the retailer, and the retailer added a profit and sold to the farmer. We received all this profit. The only cost to us of a barrel of flour was the cost of such machinery as I have described and the cost of transportation. The Brotherhood stores at that time sold all our surplus on commission. At the time of writing this—1917—the cost of producing a barrel of flour at the great Shoshone flour mills is, of course, nothing, the farm machinery, mill machinery and all devices used in connection with such manufacture being manufactured by the Association.

The facts which I have thus briefly stated must make it apparent that we were, as early as 1909, and even before that time, in a position which was entirely unassailable by competitors who had not placed themselves on a similar foundation. Our system was in a condition to challenge the whole industrial world in a free and fair field. We could and did undersell every business house in all Idaho and the competitive system, unable to compete against us, had fled from the state. Its case was hopeless. It had no footing, and never could have. It recognized capital as master and labor as its humble servant. Our system reversed the order and recognized labor as master and capital as its creature and its obedient servant. For this reason labor came to us and capital without labor was powerless. Already this condition in Idaho was affecting all adjoining states. The Co-operative system was, after ten years of honest trial, so strong, and so wondrously beautiful in its strength, that, overleaping the bounds of the co-operative state, it was infecting Oregon and Washington, and colonies framed upon the model of the Co-opolitan Association were pouring into those states. But of that I have something to say in a subsequent chapter.

CHAPTER XVIII.

PUBLICATION OF MRS. BRADEN'S NOVEL—THE PROFITS OF **THE** ASSOCIATION AND REWARD OF THE AUTHOR—THE PUBLISHING DEPARTMENT EXTENDS ITS SPHERE.

The Messenger and Publishing department, as I have previously stated, was under my especial charge. Up to the time Miss Woodberry, now Mrs. Braden, had given permission to have her novel submitted to a Co-opolitan committee, and that committee had reported favorably upon the proposition to publish it, I had conducted this department upon the most conservative lines. I confess that, even then, the vastness of the power of co-operative labor to overcome all obstacles was not fully comprehended by me. I had as yet but dimly recognized that the combined strength of labor directed to the accomplishment of a definite purpose was simply irresistible. Business in the competitive world which involves the sale and delivery of large accumulations of property, real or fictitious, is transacted upon a ridiculously narrow financial basis, and must necessarily be conducted with extreme caution. But where the fiction of money is abolished and the intercourse among men rests upon the basis of labor exchange, which is as broad as the earth itself, and as fair as perfect justice, there need be no fear of setting in motion every productive energy available. Too much of what men need or ought to have can never impoverish them.

My wife's novel was placed upon the market for sale in due season. The Daily Co-opolitan announced its appearance and contained an able and very flattering criticism of it from the pen of Mr. Edmunds. The first was a cheap edition of twenty thousand copies, and so great was the pride of all Idaho in this first literary work in the line of

THE CO-OPOLITAN. 117

fiction which could be considered distinctively Co-opolitan that the entire edition was exhausted before any could be shipped out of the state. This edition was sold for twenty cents a copy in labor-credit checks or industrial orders or money. But the demand was so great from the Brotherhood all over the country for this novel that I was compelled to have another edition of 100,000 copies struck off, and this was gotten up with so much greater ornamentation and in so much better style that I thought proper to have the price fixed at fifty cents a copy. The book had been commented upon favorably by all the newspapers and magazines of the United States and England, and not only the Brotherhood but the entire literary world was anxious to read it. The time was especially favorable to render it exceedingly popular. It was just beginning to dawn upon civilized humanity that Idaho was producing marvels in co-operative industry, and that a new civilization was born. "The West Parish" was a masterly presentation of the Co-operator's case against the competitor and had a powerful effect in convicting the latter, before the tribunal of Christian civilization, of high crimes and misdemeanors. The second edition was exhausted as swiftly, almost, as water sinks in sand. Again I was called upon to supply the unsatisfied demand of the American reader. Its high literary merit, the picture it drew of Utopia realized, the remedy it pointed out from the standard of an actual modern experience, the relief it offered to millions of starving men and women made it the sensation of the day. All classes read it. Even the conservative business man who, twenty years before, had, rather vainly, boasted that he had escaped reading "Looking Backward," quietly bought a copy of "The West Parish," and, after reading it, handed it, without comment, to his neighbor.

I now found that these two editions of the first publication of my department, in the book line, had added $40,000.00 in United States money to the accumulations of my department, and this I turned over to the Legislative Council, according to law. Again I printed an edition of one million copies. This was prepared in much cheaper style, and by advice of our Legislative Council, whose advice I had asked, I placed this edition in every book store and on every news stand in the United States at five cents a copy. This I did because it was now apparent that it was producing a great awakening among the people, and I desired, or rather, I should say, we desired, that the poor who had no means might also read. But we realized a profit even at that price, and we knew no better way to destroy the profit system than to take its profit.

We fought the devil with fire, and had a theory that if we could gain control of his fire we could extinguish it.

The million edition of "The West Parish" was taken rapidly by the class for which it was intended and the Publishing department realized the sum of $30,000.00 from that source after paying cost of transportation. I now placed an edition upon the market for standard use consisting of twenty thousand copies, finely illustrated and elegantly printed and bound. This was sold at one dollar per copy, although in the competitive system it would have been difficult for the publisher to have sold that edition on the market for three dollars a volume and to have realized a profit.

My wife's fame, of course, was now world-wide. Wherever the English language was read her name had become a household word. Her novel had also been translated into most of the languages of Europe and was working its way throughout the countries which described themselves as Christian, although more slowly than in England and the United States. The Co-opolitan Association was mindful of her incalculably great service to the cause of co-operation which it regarded as its own and at the proper time, without any department recommending it, the Legislative Council considered the propriety of offering her a reward which her work and her genius merited.

What should it be? The mechanic who invented a labor-saving device or machine, the artist whose painting had displayed extraordinary merit, the sculptor whose genius had chiseled in marble some living thought, the self-sacrifice of some hero in a moment of peril, all these merited reward, and our Association had dealt and knew how to deal with these.

But here the work had not been of moment so much because of its allurement of wealth as its supreme value as an educator. The Legislative Council considered that she was entitled to five years' release from duty as a member of the Industrial Army, and so awarded. She was entitled to this time at once and continuously, if she so notified her department chief, Mr. Edmunds, or she could give notice that she would take a portion of the time between certain dates. As a matter of fact, she chose two years' release and leave of absence commencing January 1st, 1907, and the remainder of her time later in her twenty-five years' term of service.

Having discovered the power which my department could wield, not only in Idaho, but in the world, I determined to exercise it to the fullest extent. Linotypes, electroplates and all the devices for saving labor were unsparingly employed.

I determined to put a Co-opolitan edition of all standard works of all spheres or departments, literary, scientific, religious and political, on the American market in every great city.

I began with Shakespeare. I caused an elegant edition of that immortal poet's work to be gotten up in excellent style, and sold for about two-thirds what it would cost any other house in the United States to produce. I increased my plant and followed the edition of Shakespeare in quick succession and at similarly reduced prices, with editions of all the standard English authors.

In three years' time I had Co-opolitan book stores established in Boston, New York, Philadelphia, Baltimore, Washington, Buffalo, Cincinnati, Chicago, St. Louis, St. Paul, Minneapolis, Omaha, Atlanta, New Orleans, Galveston, Denver, San Francisco, Portland and Seattle. The competitive publishing houses could not compete with our system and house after house fell before us or limited their business. I also established correspondents all through **the world and** had the latest news sent to the Co-opolitan **newspaper.**

My arrangements were **such, in conjunction with** the Brotherhood and Co-operative stores now springing up everywhere, that I had a Daily Co-opolitan issued in every one of the cities named, and the news was flashed to them daily, **as it** was to Co-opolis. I endeavored to have each Daily Co-opolitan in the hands of the national Brotherhood and each was issued on the plan of the great daily which was sent from Co-opolis to all parts of Idaho. The national Brotherhood was daily increasing in numbers and power.

My idea in extending branches of my department was to aid the national organization in destroying competition. How well I have succeeded the years have proved. The publications of the Co-opolitan Association have displaced all others and have brought millions to the safe in the basement of the Council Hall.

My department was divided in 1910 and **I was confined to** one portion called the Publishing department. A **new** department, including the messenger, telegraph, telephone and postal service, was created and Jarvis Richardson was elected its chief. I would be glad to comment upon the glorious administration of that new department, by that great and good man, but the scope of my present work does not permit. Necessarily in such a work as this I can but give the reader the most salient features of my own personal experience which tend to throw light upon the development of Idaho under the Co-opolitan control.

CHAPTER XIX.

THE STRANGER FROM LONDON—BOISE CITY BONDS AND
A LOAN—THE PERIL OF IDAHO.

The year 1906 should be considered one of the most memorable in the history of Co-operation, more on account of the great peril in which our system was placed than on account of any extraordinary undertaking. Yet perhaps I ought not to say that the year was devoid of important undertakings either, inasmuch as the Co-opolitan Transcontinental Railroad was conceived and planned that year. It was in connection with this enterprise that our peril was unwittingly incurred. The large accumulations of money which our Association was constantly making had become known to the world, so that if our Legislative Council entered upon the consideration of any great proposition the decision was looked for in financial circles, both in Wall Street, New York, and Lombard Street, London, as being a matter of prime importance. Co-opolis was now a formidable opponent and rival of those celebrated centers of competitive iniquity. Its methods were, however, the exact opposite of those of Wall Street and Lombard Street.

The proposition to construct a transcontinental railroad was particularly interesting. It was the plan of Mr. Seabury, chief of the Transportation department, to build the road in question from Co-opolis to Chicago by what he declared to be the only route which extended all the way through a productive country. This route was to parallel the Union Pacific to the Great Shoshone Falls, thence to Idaho Falls, thence veering slightly in a northerly direction to pass through the coal, iron, oil and cattle fields of Wyoming, thence entering the Black Hills region near the center, to proceed across the limestone foundation of that wonderful country, **down Rapid Valley to Rapid City, across the divide to Box Elder Valley, down that fertile valley to the Cheyenne River, down Bad River to the Missouri, over the Missouri, and thence through South Dakota, Southern Minnesota and Wisconsin to Chicago. It was also proposed that this road should be extended to Seattle, on Puget Sound.**

The plan was considered sufficiently practicable to warrant the Legislative Council to instruct the Engineering department to run preliminary surveys along the proposed route as far as the Missouri River. This order was given in the early spring; I think the records will show that it was about April 10th. A month later there appeared at the Co-opolitan Hotel an elderly gentleman who registered as Lester Hickman, London, England. Mr. Hickman appeared to be merely an English tourist. He did not, at first, make special efforts to get acquainted, but neither did he display any aversion to talking with other guests or citizens who might come in his vicinity. There was nothing about him to particularly attract attention, except that his face was very pale, his hair white, and his eyes were very gray. Perhaps they would have been very white, too, if that had been possible for keen, observing eyes. Mr. Hickman's clothes fitted him perfectly and his style of dress indicated the neat and modest gentleman. He looked the picture of scholarly innocence and spotless purity. In passing through the hotel I had noticed him several times during the week, and I had seen him on the street several times, but never felt any special curiosity as to who he might be. One day I was in my office when the young man who acted as my messenger and office attendant handed me a card, upon which was the name Lester Hickman. The attendant said the gentleman was in the anteroom and would be glad to speak with me if I was at leisure. I was at leisure and told him to show the gentleman in.

"Good afternoon, sir," said the old gentleman as he entered the door, smiling and bowing good-naturedly.

He had the air of a man whose business could not be very.

weighty, but whose motives were invariably humane. He was as white as an angel.

"Good afternoon," I returned. "Your name, I see, is Mr. Lester Hickman. I have noticed you several times about the city. What can I do for you?"

"Do not let me disturb you, sir." Mr. Hickman looked as if he could become my most intimate friend in five minutes, as he smiled patronizingly and held his hand out toward me with a gesture which seemed to indicate that he was a great man at leisure and that I was a great man whose time might be occupied. The whole manner of the man flattered me and I felt that he had my confidence at once. "I only called for information," continued he, "and do not wish to take your time, which I know is valuable."

"I am at your service, Mr. Hickman," said I. "Will you be seated?"

Mr. Hickman sat down. Even that he did with such graceful, unassuming dignity, and with such exalted deference to me, that I felt flattered again.

"You have a wonderful city, Mr. Braden," he exclaimed. "Your people have certainly built up a wonderful Commonwealth." He looked at me as he said this, as if he attributed the wonders he had seen to me.

"Yes," I replied, "The Co-opolitan has reason to be proud of his city. We have performed what has never before been achieved in nine years."

"Very true!" assented my visitor. "But you should have added, Mr. Braden, that no people ever did as much in all time." Here he smiled, and I had an undefinable feeling that he rather considered it would not have been done by the Co-opolitan Association, even, if I had not been a part of it. I found myself warming toward this sprightly, perfectly straight, white little old man wonderfully. He was either the most innocent, interesting and lovable or the most artful and cunning of men. I was inclined to think the former, but experience had taught me that such men would bear study.

"I am anxious, Mr. Braden," said Mr. Hickman, "to investigate your system of co-operation with a view to establishing a similar system in England. Some of us have a plan on foot to aid our impoverished and idle classes to gain a foothold on earth and I have been sent by my association to study Idaho. It occurred to me that you could aid me in obtaining the information I desire."

I certainly could not refuse so innocent a request, and I and my people always hastened to extend aid to such an enterprise as he described whenever it was proposed. I assured the gentleman that I would place my department at his disposal and recommended him to see Mr. Edmunds of the Educational department. The latter would place our historical records at his disposal and he would gain, from that source, the fullest information.

This white gentleman remained with me nearly an hour. A more entertaining conversationalist it has rarely been my fortune to meet. He had traveled extensively, was acquainted with most of the famous men of England, and the moral tone of his conversation was the highest conceivable.

"There is only one thing I notice about your system which I cannot approve," said he. "Your Association has pursued a course calculated to destroy the value of all the public bonds in Idaho except those of the state. There are Boise City municipal bonds, for instance, which have no value in the market because you have constructed a magnificent co-operative city outside the territory affected by them. I do not see how you can escape the charge of immorality in refusing to pay them."

These remarks were made by the white saint with such apparent sincerity that I did not at that time doubt they sprang from an honest heart. I met him many times after and he never referred to that subject again. He remained in Co-opolis three months, during which time he was a constant attendant upon church and I observed that he was often to be seen in the company of the members of the ministry. Just before he departed he called upon the Legislative Council, then in session, and asked to make a statement to that body. The **request was** granted and he spoke briefly. He said he **understood that** the Legislative Council was considering plans **for the** construction of a transcontinental railroad, that he understood the Association was not then prepared to **build the** road, but would be obliged to **defer** the **completion of it** until its finances permitted; **that** he was acquainted **with** numerous philanthropic gentlemen in England who **were** much interested in Co-opolitan success; that he was **able** to procure from these **gentlemen a loan of** one million pounds sterling for the **Association, at the nominal** rate of three per cent interest **per annum, the bonds to run** for twenty years; that he **would use his best** endeavors to accomplish this purpose, providing **the Association** would agree to purchase at the end of that **time the** outstanding municipal bonds of the various cities for fifty cents on the dollar. He said he had no knowledge as to who might be the owners of such bonds, but for the good name of the Association he desired to **urge** that this course be pursued.

The Legislative Council paid **very little** attention to this proposal, at that time, ascribing **it to the** gentleman's ignorance of our system.

Mr. Hickman had **not been** gone a week before I made a discovery which startled me. I found that a petition was being circulated, under our Association law, asking the President of the Association to **submit** three laws, which were attached to the petition, to the people, to be voted upon at the next October election. What appalled me most was **that they were** being circulated by the clergy, who went **from house to house** for the purpose.

The **first** provided that the Association **borrow $5,000,-000.00 for** the purpose of constructing **a** transcontinental railroad **and** issue bonds on such road bearing three per cent interest **per** annum **and** running for twenty years. The second recited the moral obligation of the Association to assume certain municipal bonds which had become valueless and to pay for the same, setting forth also the fact that as long as these bonds remained unpaid the territory formerly occupied by the cities of Lewiston, Boise, Ketchem, Shoshone and several others would be valueless. It then provided that the Association pay for these bonds at the rate of fifty cents on the dollar in five years from the passage of the law. The third provided that all industrial orders be retired and that all labor be paid for after January 1st, 1907, by labor checks which would be non-transferable.

While these three laws were to be submitted separately for the voters to pass upon, they were attached to one petition. The law permitted this action at that time, but as soon as possible after this abuse was discovered the Legislative Council corrected the plain defect so that each law must be supported by a separate petition in order to obtain a reference to the people, and the correction was so obviously proper that it has ever since remained the law.

I made no doubt when I saw this petition that the white saint-like personage, Lester Hickman, was an agent of some English syndicate, and that this whole scheme had been set on foot by him to get the municipal bonds of these several cities paid.

Some time after I learned that I was correct in this surmise. His syndicate had procured the bonds referred to for a mere nominal sum, and hit upon the plan of loaning the Association $5,000,000.00 and getting the bonds paid at the same time. As for the proposed loan, it would have been as safe as the bonds of the nation, and the entire financial world so regarded it. Why not? The Co-opolitan Association was absolutely solvent and was looked upon as enormously rich.

Hickman was a shrewd agent. He had amassed great wealth for himself, and was as artful as any living man in inducing men to part with the fruits of their industry without receiving due compensation. In approaching the Co-opolitan Association he donned the sheep's clothing of an adviser and advocate of co-operation, and went immediately to the ministry and preached morality. With them he succeeded.

Those who best understood the theory of morals and

could preach it in all its purity were least able to discriminate between the spurious and the real. Hickman belonged to a class of artful tempters who have done more to enslave mankind and degrade morals than any other. Members of this class go forth daily from our great cities to lobby in legislative bodies, bribe judges, corrupt city councils and induce the representatives of the people to give away valuable public privileges or part with public utilities.

In Co-opolis Hickman enlisted the clergy by making large donations to the churches, talking to them about a high standard of morality which he professed, claiming to be entirely disinterested and assuming a modest and retiring piety. He was a financial Talleyrand.

The result of Hickman's efforts was that after he was gone, and almost before we knew what was going on, the petition containing thirty thousand names of members of the Association was sent to the President. This was not twenty per cent of the population of the state, but at that time all Co-operators were not members of the Co-opolitan Association. There were several distinct associations, embracing in their membership a total of nearly forty thousand. There were, besides, some thirty thousand who were not members of any association. Three years later all co-operative associations in the state were received into the Co-opolitan Association, and the individualists who still declined to become identified with our organization were few. But at the time the petitions in question were presented the thirty thousand names affixed to them constituted twenty per cent of the total vote of the Co-opolitan Association.

Here then issue was joined. However impatient our chief officers might feel with the Co-operators who had imprudently and unwisely raised these serious questions, or at least the bond and credit questions, there was no alternative and the duty to refer them to the popular vote was imperative. Some of us felt that it was a great misfortune, and I confess that I trembled for the result. Let me say now, as a candid man, that I have never been very sanguine of the success of any issue which was left to the popular decision, except on the one occasion when I felt faith in the successful establishment of the co-operative programme in 1902.

My faith even then rested upon a theory that the masses will sometimes do right impulsively and err when they stop to deliberate. As a candid man, I am also bound to say that experience proves my suspicions to have been unfounded in every instance. Our referendum law was, and is, in one respect, superior to that of Switzerland. It provided then, as now, that proposed laws should be published for a period of six weeks at least, but, in addition, it very wisely denied to any member the right to vote unless he had attended three public debates in which the law to be voted on was discussed. Our method then, as now, was to appoint certain days for such discussions, and we selected the ablest disputants on both sides of the question at issue to fully present the arguments on their respective sides in joint debate. In this manner the people became fully informed. These disputants were generally recommended then, as now, by the partisans of one or the other theory, but if no recommendation was made the Association appointed an able and learned man to represent the defaulting side.

No political party has ever existed in Idaho since 1905. Men have combined on numerous occasions the better to support their convictions with regard to certain proposed laws; but the men who honestly agreed on one proposition were just as likely to honestly disagree as to the next question. So that each organization was at an end when its mission was acomplished. Moreover, as all are provided for, there is no occasion to form parties to secure political office.

CHAPTER XX.

THE DEBATE ON THE BOND AND CREDIT LAWS—REV. CADMUS M. DESTY AND THE MORAL LAW.

The discussion of the bond and credit laws referred to the people to be voted upon at the Association election in October, 1907, was as earnest, interesting and thorough as any which had ever occurred in Idaho. The advocates of their adoption were vigorous and persistent and regarded themselves as conscientious.

They were not honest, however, with themselves. They had allowed an artful and unscrupulous agent of the competitive system to convince them that a moral question was involved and to delude them into believing him to be a great and good man.

Indeed, Hickman had written a pamphlet on "Co-operation and Financial Integrity," which was published on his return to New York City from Co-opolis, and a large number of these had been sent back to Co-opolis and distributed throughout Idaho.

It was an able presentation of the view he desired his partisans in Idaho to urge. It was not his view, however, but simply the plea which a shrewd lawyer in the competitive world might make for a guilty criminal. It was sufficiently effective to become the text-book of the affirmative in the discussion, and they lauded Hickman to the skies until it was proven that he had for years been the trusted agent of the celebrated banking house of Rothschild. After that the bond advocate mentioned Hickman no more.

In this discussion every member of the Legislative Council of the Association and every member of the Great Council were enlisted in opposition to these laws. Ex-Governor, now United States Senator, Thompson was one of the most active of the negative speakers. On the side of the affirmative was the Reverend Dr. Cadmus M. Desty, the famous pulpit orator, a most conscientious man and an intelligent Co-operator. He had become convinced, and I would stake life itself that he was perfectly honest in the matter, that our whole system must fail if we broke what he conceived to be God's law, and did what was unjust and dishonest.

The whole basis of his contention was the moral law. He was an emotional speaker. It was his custom to support his views by making copious quotations from the bible and, drawing from them some conclusions which were satisfactory to his mind, launch into an exhortation which was perfectly irresistible to some of his emotional followers.

In those days our discussions were not conducted as they are to-day. Then the disputants were given an hour or an hour and a half each to present his side. Our system of requiring the affirmative to state an argument in ten minutes, and the negative to reply in the same length of time, continuing in this manner for several hours in the presence of referees who permit no divergence from the subject, is calculated to exclude oratory and passion, and raise the discussion to an intellectual plane. But the system was not adopted until 1912.

It must be confessed that the oratorical contests of the old style were as interesting as a circus or gladiatorial show, in which respect they were superior to the give-and-take method of to-day.

The greatest of all the debates of that campaign occurred between Senator Thompson and the Reverend Dr. Desty during September. One of these took place in the great hall at Co-opolis. There were present 9,000 members of the Industrial Army and one thousand pupils from the schools. It was our custom to have the Educational department send a certain number of its wards to these discussions, in order to have them familiarized with Co-opolitan methods. These questions were always discussed fully in the schools as well as in the Industrial Army.

The discussion in the great hall was opened by Dr. Desty.

He insisted that the bonds of Boise City should be paid, that the poor people, who doubtless held them, factory operators in the unfortunate competitive cities, perhaps, had purchased them in good faith; that the action of the Co-opolitan Association, which he entirely approved, had rendered these bonds valueless, and that the Association, which was founded on principles of justice, equality and righteousness, should not withhold from these poor people what belonged to them.

He also pointed out the fact that as long as the bonds remained outstanding the territory affected by them would be lost to the Association. Then came the wonderful, soul-stirring oratory of the man, which moved his hearers to the depths. I almost felt, as I listened to him on that occasion, that perhaps he was right.

When he finished the applause from all parts of the hall was deafening. I believe now that it was more an acknowledgment of his wonderful oratory than because he had produced a conviction of the correctness of his views, but I was distressed by different thoughts then.

Senator Thompson followed on behalf of the negative. The Senator was at that time in the very prime of an exceptionally strong and vigorous manhood. He had occupied the important positions of President of the Association and Governor of the state, the former for seven years, the latter for two. His reputation was world-wide, not as an orator, but as the father of the Co-operative Commonwealth and the possessor of extraordinary administrative ability. He had not, as yet, taken his oath of Senator of the United States, having been but recently elected, and was hardly known as a public speaker outside of the state. He was not an emotional orator.

His chief characteristics in debate were his ready wit, his complete command of the subject under discussion, and his logical and powerful array of facts. He was the opposite of the Reverend Dr. Desty in nearly every respect. That day he was at his best. As he came forward to the speakers' stand he was received with terrific applause. This was always the case, however, and it did not indicate that his was the most popular side.

He commenced by informing the audience that he did not desire to use any personal influence with them concerning the exercise of their suffrage. He wished them to be guided by truth and wisdom only. If the people of Idaho were not sufficiently intelligent to save their Co-operative Commonwealth then it must fall, because their intelligence was its sole foundation. He had some evidence to present for their consideration.

Here he read three affidavits from England, which set forth the business, character and history of one Lester Hickman. These averred that gentleman to be the president of the American and English Bond and Trust Company, limited, of London, and that his company was the purchaser, for a mere nominal sum, of the municipal bonds of the cities of Idaho. They further averred that Hickman was known as a bitter enemy of all movements for the bettering of the condition of the people, and neither more nor less than a keen broker and speculator. They also set forth that Hickman's reputation for honesty was somewhat shady.

After reading these affidavits Senator Thompson exclaimed:

"This is the prophet of financial morality whose teachings are invoked for your instruction by my good and sincere but misguided friend, Dr. Desty." At this point the applause which shook the house and was again and again repeated marked the turning of the tide of public sentiment against the affirmative.

"I think now," resumed the Senator, after quiet was restored, "that the bond and credit laws are dead. But I would not have you decide this question on the simple fact that the man who instigated them is a selfish hypocrite and schemer. I want you to understand these laws thoroughly and adopt or reject them on their merits. If they are good, it matters not who proposes them. Let them be adopted.

If they are bad, it matters not what demon inspired them, they should be rejected.

"These laws are for what purpose? To introduce among you the most iniquitous feature of the competitive system.

"Once allow it to be introduced, whether under the guise of necessity or morality, whether by Shylock or by an erring angel, and I would not give a straw for your entire system. It will eat its way into the very heart of your body politic and destroy all that is worth having about it.

"History shows to my mind successive systems of slavery, one chasing the other through the earth.

"Bond slavery succeeded chattel slavery and has nearly crushed liberty to death in the great republic. There is not the slightest reason why the Co-opolitan Association should become indebted to private persons.

"We are the public, the law, the will of Idaho, and what we desire within the state that we can have. If we wish to build a railroad beyond the state we ought to have no difficulty in doing that.

"What is necessary to such a road? First you must have the line surveyed. That has been done. Next you must have the right of way. That will be somewhat expensive. But if the right of way costs us five million dollars why should we borrow it? We have it already. Even if we did not have it, let me remind you that from 1862 to 1892, a period of thirty years, Idaho produced nearly two hundred million dollars of gold and silver, and her producing population was at no time greater than thirty thousand persons. With a population such as we have to-day we can produce gold enough, if gold is needed, in a single year, to build this road.

"Would not Idaho be demented to borrow gold from a hypocritical agent of Rothschild when we can, without incurring debt, take it from our own valleys, creek beds and mountains?"

The Senator treated the question of bond issues from every point of view conceivable, with a power of description, illustration and argument that not only held his audience spellbound, but fixed its logic deep in the minds of all who heard him. Such was the effect of the affidavits which he read upon the mind of his reverend opponent that the latter declared his intention never again to enter upon the discussion of political questions or questions of public finance. Thenceforth he confined himself to religion and became a world-renowned pulpit orator.

When the election occurred the vote was overwhelming against all these laws, the last going down largely on account of the unpopularity of the two others known as the land and credit propositions. Our system did not permit the submission of a rejected law for at least five years after its rejection. The proposition to abolish the labor orders and pay all labor in non-transferable checks was a really meritorious one and ought to have been adopted.

The people, however, are so constituted that once their suspicions are aroused they are much readier to say no than yes, and the abolition of orders as a medium of labor exchange had to wait until 1912. It is gratifying, however, to be able to say that the people were less and less inclined to demand such orders, and more and more inclined to receive the labor checks.

The defeat of the bond and credit laws had the effect of placing the Co-opolitan Association and the co-operative system on an enduring basis. The entire world now realized that it was an assured and successful system and in every state in the Union the tendency was toward the enactment of laws favorable to co-operative action on the part of the laborer. Nearly all the states, seized by the spirit of the hour, began to discuss the propriety of calling a constitutional convention and reforming their systems of state government upon the model of Idaho.

The features of our state constitution most favored were its provisions embodying the initiative and referendum and the imperative mandate, which I have already described.

CHAPTER XXI.

WHY IDAHO HAS A DUAL GOVERNMENT—A GLIMPSE AT THE LAW.

The second Governor of Idaho and the second President of the Co-opolitan Association, succeeding Senator Thompson to both positions, was Hon. Henry B. Henderson. The political machinery of the state was in the control of the Association and our policy was to make the executive officers of the Association the executive officers of the state also. Some of those readers who live beyond the boundaries of Idaho into whose hands this history may come do not comprehend why we continued to run two organizations in the name of the people, instead of one. They are, perhaps, at a loss to understand why the Co-opolitan Association did not, when it had acquired nearly all the land in Idaho and embraced nearly all the population of the state, transfer its dominion to the state government and operate its co-operative system as a state institution. The reason is simple enough. The state was necessarily limited in its powers by the Federal constitution. There were several very important functions which were by that instrument denied to state governments, but not to private corporations, and we desired to exercise them.

I have already adverted to the fact that the Federal constitution prohibits the state from issuing "bills of credit." This does not prevent corporations, associations or private persons from doing so. When we dealt with the commercial world "bills of credit" were often necessary. Moreover, our industrial orders might be construed to be bills of credit and this plan of labor exchange was, in reality, one of the most important features of our co-operative system. If the state had inaugurated such a plan the Federal prohibition would have crushed it at once.

Still another important power would have been lost had the state government owned and operated our system. We could not have extended our business into any other state in the Union. It was our purpose to build railroads. Most of the states permitted a corporation organized in another state for that purpose to build railroads within their limits and take land for their right of way by right of eminent domain. No state had a law upon its statute books which gave similar powers to another state. It had never been contemplated that a state would do business or own railroads within its own limits, much less within the limits of another state.

The Co-opolitan Association was organized under the laws of Idaho. There the Association did not so much conform to the laws as the laws conformed to the needs of the Association. This dual system proved to be extremely useful. We made the state perform police duties for us and regulate the relation of our members to one another. We had a system of courts regulated by state law, but these had little to do. In 1910 we repealed the laws giving remedies for the collection of any debt or the enforcement of any contract entered into after January 1st, 1911, except against the Co-opolitan Association. We had a criminal code and punished crimes, but the people were all provided for and educated, so that three great causes of crime—poverty, excessive wealth and ignorance—being minimized, the criminal courts had little to do. That other cause of crimes—drunkenness—is uncommon. All alcoholic or intoxicating drinks were not only sold by the Association, but were of the purest quality. It was and is a crime to import any liquors into the state for sale, but the Association is its own manufacturer.

CHAPTER XXII.

THE STATE GOVERNMENT—ITS INSANE, WEAK-MINDED BLIND, SICK, AGED AND INFIRM—THE INDUSTRIAL ARMY—ITS ORGANIZATION AND PRODUCTIVE POWER.

All the labor of the state of Idaho was, as early as 1910, performed exclusively by the Industrial Army of the **Co-opolitan Association.** We had intended at the **outset of** our career to transfer all our property to the state government when it should come under our control, but for the reasons already mentioned that plan was abandoned. Even as late as the year following the adoption of our Co-operative institution we expected to pursue that course. But as soon as we began the actual work of legislation we discovered that the better and simpler method, and one which rendered it easier to avoid conflict with the Federal constitution, was to keep the state government within very narrow limits. As a result the state government delegated all its important functions which could be delegated to the Co-opolitan Association. Its Great Council still continued to exercise its legislative and judicial functions and the executive still continued to act as the chief police and military officer. But the state government was hardly **more than a bridge** connecting the Co-operative state with the Federal Constitution. The latter could not recognize **the** former, but the state government could, and did. **The** state complied **with** the constitution of the country as **a** political organism. The Co-opolitan Association, as the industrial, financial, social and commercial organism, did as it pleased. Notwithstanding all **this, the** Co-operative state, the state of Idaho and the **Co-opolitan Association** were **one** and the same, and the **last-mentioned,** embracing all **the** people of the state and its **membership,** was the living and controlling power in and **behind the whole.**

We had expected that the state of Idaho would have an Industrial Army of its own. Experience, however, convinced us that it would be far better to do all its work through the Association. Insane, weak-minded, blind, sick, aged and infirm persons who were members of the Association were cared for by the Association, so that the state had no duty to perform toward them. The children of our members inherited membership, losing it only by violating its laws in some few particulars, so that insane, weak-minded, sick or infirm children of members were all cared for. To care for persons who might be afflicted, however, and were not members of the Association was the state's concern. To punish criminals was its duty. The Great Council contracted with the Co-opolitan Association to care for its afflicted and its criminals, and the sole consideration which it charged for this burden was that it have the benefit of the labor of the able-bodied among them.

We soon found that the criminals whom the state consigned to our care, when given a fair opportunity, were most of them able and willing to work. This was all the more apparent when we offered a reward, consisting of wages equal to a Co-opolitan's dividend, for meritorious conduct. We rarely ever permitted a convict to become a member of our Industrial Army, however meritorious his work, but we did not oblige him to quit our service on the penitential farm or in the penitential factories when his term of service expired. Yet we did admit Barnstead, who invented a flying machine; Applegate, the inventor of the electric plough; Turner, that poet who sang with wonderful power the songs of Remorse, Injustice and Sorrow, and some thirty others. The state criminal is now almost a thing of the past, yet fifteen years ago our penitential farms and factories were important concerns. But we made them pay. They produced not only enough wealth to support themselves substantially, but enough to support the state insane, weak-minded, sick, aged and infirm, whose several asylums adjoined the farms.

Our Industrial Army in that year—1910—contained

twenty-four **departments, in which** 1,025,525 persons **were at** that time **enlisted. Of these** four hundred and sixty-two thousand one hundred and twenty-one were women. It was a magnificent body of well-trained, intelligent, earnest, industrious and faithful men and **women.** The chief of this **body was** the President of **the** Association. Its movements **were** directed by the Legislative Council. Its general laws were enacted by that body, but each department **and** subdivision had regulations of its own which did not conflict with those provided by the Legislative Council. There were then twenty-five **general** departments, as follows:

1st. Department of Agriculture. All occupations requiring the cultivation of the soil, except such as were within the Nursery and Fruit department, were within its province.

2nd. The Live Stock department had charge of all cattle, **horses,** sheep, **hogs** and other animals, as well as birds.

3rd. The Nursery and Fruit department had charge **of** all orchards, vines and plants bearing fruit **and** all horticultural plants and flowers.

4th. The Irrigation department **had charge** of all waters and the distribution of the same.

5th. The Commerce department **had** charge of all department stores and was charged, as **now,** with supplying the needs of the people.

6th. The Manufacturing department had charge **of all** factories and all manufactures.

7th. The Transportation department had charge of all highways, methods of transportation, vehicles and the operation of the same.

8th. The Messenger and Publishing department had charge of the means and instrumentalities of communication and publication, including telegraphs, telephones, signals, newspapers and magazines.

9th. The Educational department had charge of the education **of** the young.

10th. The Department of Public Amusements had charge of the entertainment of the people.

11th. The Department of Health had charge of the public health, the care, treatment and cure of the sick and the burial of the dead. Also all hospitals, sanitariums, mineral springs, medicines, drugs and medical practice.

12th. The Legal department had charge of the legal business of the Association. This department employed about one hundred and fifty persons in 1910.

13th. The Timber and Forestry department had charge of the timber and saw mills of the Association. It was also charged with the preservation of the forest.

14th. The Labor department had charge of the unclassified labor of the Association. From the Educational department all students passed into this department, where they were generally required to serve three years. All persons enlisting who did not possess a trade or evince some special aptitude were also generally assigned to this department. Advancement to other departments, or the official positions in this one, were the rewards of merit. This department was also required to find constant employment for its forces or to report forthwith to the Legislative Council its failure to do so. In the latter case the Legislative Council would cause new enterprises to be undertaken.

15th. The Department of Public Improvements was charged with the investigation of all plans for new roads, parks, waterways and the improvements of the methods, conveniences and comforts of the people. Plans or ideas were received by this department from any person and whenever a plan or idea was accepted, provided it was new, original and meritorious, a reward in the form of a vacation was given the originator.

16th. The Department of Invention was charged with the duty of searching out, investigating, testing and introducing all labor-saving inventions to the Association. This proved to be one of the most useful departments. Manufacturers are not usually able to find time to experiment and are generally averse to introducing new machinery or methods. This department did all the work of experimenting and reported results.

17th. The Department of Art had charge of all decorating, painting, drawing, sculpture, architecture, designing, etc.

18th. The Engineering department had charge of all engineering work.

19th. The Department of Building not only had charge of all buildings and was responsible for their healthfulness and security, but was the manufacturer of all building material, except lumber, and quarried all stone employed by it or shipped to another state. The granite, white calico and lilac mottled marble, the gypsum, sandstone and other building stone, as well as ornamental onyx stone, produced by our quarries, were, and still are, handled by this department.

20th. The Department of Mining had charge of all the mining except coal.

21st. The Land department had charge of all the unused lands of the Association.

22d. The Food department had charge of the preparation and distribution of all foods at public or private tables, the killing, dressing and packing or canning of meats, and the preparation, preserving or canning of fruits, vegetables and other edibles.

23d. The Department of Fuel, Heat and Light had charge of all heating and lighting plants and all sources of fuel, such as coal mines, gas wells and oil wells.

24th. The Department of Science had charge of the scientific investigation, of the geology, mineralogy and natural resources of the state and their chemical analysis.

25th. The Department of Accounts and Statistics was then, as now, the Auditory department. In addition to this it received and transmitted all orders between the departments. For instance, if the flour section of the department store desired flour the Commerce department must send its orders to the Department of Accounts and Statistics. Here the order is recorded and immediately transmitted to the Manufacturing department. If the Manufacturing department has no flour it transmits an order to this department for wheat, which is recorded and transmitted to the Agricultural department. When the order for wheat is filled this department is notified by the department filling and that receiving, and so with the flour when delivered. This department also keeps a full record of all the property and products of the Association.

These several departments were again subdivided by the Legislative Council into divisions and sections.

Our method of co-operation, through the instrumentality of the Industrial Army, resulted in our being able to produce more than three times as much wealth each year as an equal population usually did in the competitive system.

The population of the state at that time, including men, women and children, was 3,160,000. Such a population in a competitive state will contain about five thousand lawyers.

We had one hundred and fifty lawyers and four thousand eight hundred and fifty strong men in our producing ranks. The wives of these men were also in our Industrial Army.

Such a population in competition usually supports six thousand saloon men and bartenders. Liquors were sold in the various department stores of the Association at that time and in the restaurants and hotels, but there were no bars and no saloons. They were handled incidentally with drugs, medicines or foods. In the competitive system the liquor dealers and bartenders form a special force. The liquors in Idaho were dispensed by the clerks and waiters who handled other goods. We could safely count six thousand workers in our Industrial Army aiding in the production of wealth instead of six thousand saloon men and bartenders.

Instead of eight thousand claim, commission, real estate and insurance agents and collectors we had an equal number of men at work in our factories, on our farms, or in the distributing departments.

The restaurant and hotel keepers, brokers, commercial

travelers, hucksters and peddlers and merchants in such a population in a competitive state would number sixty thousand. All these, instead of preying upon us and consuming the fruits of our labor without giving any return for it, were now at work with us.

Body and personal servants who wait upon the rich in a state of three million inhabitants will number in the neighborhood of ninety thousand, and all these were in our Industrial Army helping to increase the annual wealth of the state.

We had no gamblers, professional capitalists, speculators or leisure classes in 1910, but we had an equal number of honest workers.

We were not compelled to waste time in searching for employment, hunting for customers or waiting for trade.

We were not distressed by the pressure of a few overburdened and a large number who could get neither the burden nor the reward for carrying it.

There were no overdone trades and no overstocked markets.

Wherever we found power, whether human, natural or mechanical, we sought to employ it.

Two incentives were furnished by the Association to honest and diligent effort on the part of the worker. The first was promotion to a higher grade. The second was a reward in the nature of a leave of absence. These incentives were powerful, especially as Idaho, being one of the most beautiful and picturesque states in the Union and abounding in game, offered an inviting field for recreation. But another force was also at work among the men and women of the Army. Each felt that he was a partner in this great enterprise. Each regarded the idler who "stole time" as his foe. Each was determined that the other should do his duty, and the laggard and loafer was regarded with such contempt by his associates that no one cared to incur the odium of that reputation. This had a very pronounced effect both as to the quality and quantity of the work done.

At and before that time I had noticed that a large number of those who entered the Army from other states were actuated by a desire to earn the large dividends paid to members for several years, cash their checks or orders and withdraw. In a few instances only have I noticed that these intentions were carried out.

Such persons found that in our system they were able to obtain all the best fruits of competition without the worry, distress and mockery of that system. Their labor was better rewarded, their hours of toil were shorter, they were never confronted by want, they were called upon to divide with neither poverty nor distress; they were equal to the best as far as material things were concerned and they were not superior to any one in those respects. I remember that a few were, or affected to be, distressed because they could not own any real estate. But in a few months they realized that they would never be disturbed in the possession of the house they occupied as long as it satisfied them, and that, should sickness or death come, their families were safe.

When a workman was injured or fell sick his dividend was paid as fully as if he were at work. If injured by accident or negligence he had no remedy, although the person responsible for his injury might suffer punishment. His assurance of receiving his membership dividends was sufficient comfort.

If the worker urged that he should have a vested right in the Association property, above the share of its annual earnings, it was only necessary to remind him that in the competitive system he would never think of demanding of his employer a similar share, and was generally compelled to be satisfied with a pittance for wages. In the co-operative system he received his dividend, which represented, in 1910, twelve hundred dollars per annum, purchased everything he needed cheaper than competition ever made it for him, was insured against accident or sickness, had his family protected against his death, was furnished educational facilities and positions for his children, and was more certainly a part of the governing power than he could be under any constitution. Instead of being the hunted victim of a hundred ingenious **robbers** who flattered him with **the** promise that he would strengthen his individuality by permitting them **to** chase and starve him and his family, he discovered that his individuality improved with prosperity and his confidence and courage rose in an equal and healthy contest.

CHAPTER XXIII.

THE TRANSCONTINENTAL RAILROAD.

The Co-opolitan Transcontinental Railroad was completed in 1910 to Chicago. Two years before that the last spike had been driven at Seattle, on Puget Sound, and trains had since been running regularly on that portion of the road. The construction of the road through Washington, Wyoming and South Dakota was not interrupted by any obstacles or opposition. Indeed, the people of those states offered every inducement for us to pass through their country.

When we reached the Black Hills in South Dakota we found the route from Silver City to Rapid City down the narrow valley of Rapid Creek occupied by a partially completed railroad which the projector had been compelled to abandon for lack of funds. This we purchased for a small sum. With that exception the right of way through Washington, Wyoming and South Dakota cost us practically nothing. Moreover, the farmers in Eastern South Dakota aided us with their labor, accepting the produce and merchandise which we brought with us from Idaho for pay. The labor orders, also, were in demand along that part of our road, and we established the department stores in the states where these orders were soon received back for wares.

The state of Washington was at the time our road reached Seattle largely under the control of the Washington Co-operative Association, and that Association, being like the Co-opolitan, a creature of the National Brotherhood of the Co-operative Commonwealth, deemed its interests identical with ours and aided us materially in pushing our enterprise in that direction.

In Minnesota, Wisconsin and Illinois the several legislatures had denied to all, except domestic corporations, the right to exercise the power of eminent domain. This law had been passed at recent sessions of their legislatures at the instance of certain railroad companies to exclude our line. The people of these several states had been much incensed when the laws mentioned were enacted. Had the initiative and referendum been in force there as in Idaho this would not have been a serious impediment. We could then have gone among the indignant citizens and procured a petition signed by twenty per cent of the voters of the state asking that the obnoxious laws be submitted to the popular vote.

Such was the feeling against the corrupt corporations at the time that people would have hastened to sign such a petition. But they had no initiative and referendum law, and so were at the mercy of the corruptionists.

The plain reason why the competing railroads desired to exclude our line, and why the farmers desired to have it enter these states, was the understanding that we would reduce all rates, both passenger and freight, to the great advantage of the farmers.

In fact, we designed to make a reduction in these respects which would mean ruin for all competing lines.

We were able to do this.

In the first place the road had cost us nothing but labor, except what we paid in cash to purchase the Rapid Valley Road and the right of way over the lands of certain hostile farmers. Even this cash represented our labor and was valuable only as it would purchase other labor or its products.

Then the competitive roads had been enormously expensive to build. The projectors were compelled, when they proposed their enterprises, to bribe a large number of so-called capitalists to advance money which had doubtless been intrusted to them by laborers for investment. Such capitalists, having little they could call their own, must needs obtain it.

So these railroad builders and their financiers placed

side by side with the genuine million won from labor **a false and pretended million which** had its inception in **and** owed its existence to fraud. Then the true and false were made to pass together, **with extended hands** demanding **of** the toiler a portion of **his** product as **their lawful dues.** The one was just, **the other a fiction and a sham.**

False stock, which never had any basis **in labor;** false bonds, which had no mission except to defraud labor of its product; false pretenses, which made it possible for knaves to live by their wits, were the excuses which capitalists put forth for those extortionate rates **by** which the people were impoverished.

Our railroad represented no such presumptuous and dastardly pretensions. We came as labor should come to labor, asking no more and no less than labor's honest dues.

No stock, no bonds, no fraudulent construction companies came with us. We did not deal in dollars nor peddle securities.

We had naught but labor **to expend, and pretended nothing** more. But we had **all that labor makes and thousands of** willing hands.

When **we built our road we offered it for use as the** creature **of** labor and not the creature **of capital.**

To **build** it and equip it we began **at** the very foundation. The ore we mined, and smelted it in our own furnaces. We fashioned our own plough and **with** it turned the furrow. We made the harrow and followed it afield. We planted the grain and when it ripened in the golden sun we harvested it with blades our own hands wrought. We delved again, and from the mines we brought the ore, and in the blazing furnaces we moulded the steel automata which, at our bidding, amid the Shoshone's roar, reduced our wheat to flour, or wove the wool **of our own** flocks to cloth.

Then **we** made **rails of steel,** and of the pulp of straw made paper ties, and threw up grades, or hewed our way through rock-ribbed hills. And so our road was built to Minnesota's line and **we** proposed **to** build it through that state and onward **to Chicago.**

It can be seen that our own road could, when completed, be operated far cheaper than any of the competitive class. We had our coal in Idaho at first cost; our iron at first cost; our steel rails, ties and all necessary equipments at first cost. No brokers or speculators intervened.

Our railroad force wore clothing which we made, and no retailer exacted from our employe a profit. We fed him with our own home-grown and home-made flour, sugar, beef and supplies. How could the competitors compete with that?

We did not delay long at Minnesota's boundary. The Brotherhood in that state soon organized a company under the laws of the state and its stock was nearly all conveyed to our Association, except just enough to enable us to have nominal officers in the state as the law required. The same course was pursued in Wisconsin and Illinois and our road was completed in due time.

Similar consequences followed the completion of this road that followed the establishment of our department store and hotel at Boise City.

The business of nearly all the roads to the coast came to the Co-opolitan. The other roads could not compete with us.

We reduced our rates to one cent a mile. The other roads followed suit, supposing it possible for them to force us to terms.

The Legislative Council thereupon placed the fare at one dollar for the through trip from any point along the line to Seattle and one cent per mile for any distance less than one hundred miles. This was continued for two years without any change and the travel on the road was enormous and profitable at that price.

Freight rates were also reduced. The result of this road as to the manufactures of Idaho was to give them a "boom."

Our woolen goods were especially salable. We had over four million sheep in Idaho and our woolen mills were consuming all the wool yield and that of Washington, Oregon and Montana. These goods were of superior quality and we were able to sell them cheaper than English manufacturers could without a tariff.

Two years before our road was completed to Chicago, after the last spike was driven at Seattle, we began the construction in that city of three large buildings costing one million dollars each.

These were of the most magnificent character and were equal to anything which in the competitive system would have compelled us to spend four or five million each. The reason was that we furnished the stone, slate, marble, lime and all building material from Idaho and performed all the work with our own Co-opolitan labor. We also transported men and material on our railroad.

One of these buildings was a co-operative store, another a co-operative hotel and a third a Palace of Amusements. This supplied Seattle with all needed in the way of clothing, food, hotel entertainment or accommodation and amusement or recreation, and constituted that combination by which we had successfully defeated all industrial or competitive opposition in Idaho.

The Washington Co-operative Association had arranged with us that we should be allowed Seattle as our seaport town, and we proceeded to establish a steamship line with China and Japan and arranged for other lines to countries bordering on the Pacific Ocean. This we had no difficulty in doing, as we had gold and silver in large quantities, taken from our mines or won from competitors, with which to deal with the barbarous people who use them.

As for Seattle, it had long been inclined to co-operation. Its business men and citizens had been for years struggling against every conceivable disadvantage and were completely at the mercy of trusts and combinations of the most unconscionable character. They had been approaching closer and closer to bankruptcy day by day until our "Three Brothers," as they called the hotel, department store and amusement hall, received them into their fraternal arms.

Since Seattle became a co-operative city it has grown to be the great Pacific seaport of the co-operative world. Its widened avenues, its magnificent parks, its comfortable cottages, its great wharves and piers, its forest of masts, its magnificent Industrial Army, its schools and institutions of learning all bespeak a prosperity which is the pride of her citizens. And this pride is all the more excusable because the Seattle of to-day is the property of all her citizens and not the property of a few.

CHAPTER XXIV.

CHARLIE WOODBERRY ASKS QUESTIONS.

We were seated on the veranda of my house on Salem Avenue. It was a summer evening after tea in 1912. My wife sat by my side and her brother, Charlie Woodberry, a young man about twenty-two, sat with us. My little daughter and a number of children about her own age played upon the lawn in front of the house.

The day had been an exceedingly hot one—such a day as the farmers say is excellent for corn—but the evening was cool and delightful, as all the evenings are in Idaho.

We were engaged in watching the children as they played and listening to their merry laughter. As the evening wore on and the dusk deepened into darkness, when the little girl, tired of play, came and sat in her little chair on the veranda, our conversation took a more serious turn.

Charlie was a visitor from Fall River, Massachusetts, and in that city was employed in the office of a large factory in the capacity of bookkeeper. I think his salary was at that time about eighty dollars per month. He was spending his three weeks' vacation with us.

"Mr. Braden," said he, "I learned to-day that your book 'Co-operative Economy' is probably responsible for your being Governor of Idaho and President of the Association. I have never read it, but my two days' visit in Co-opolis makes me anxious to read it."

"Yes," I replied. "Probably the book did have more to do with my selection than anything else. I certainly hope you will read it, because I have endeavored in that book to explain the whole co-operative system as industrially applied in this state, and, while you will hardly read it for pleasure, you will understand our system better if you study it."

The term of President Henderson of Co-opolis had expired the year before and I had been selected to succeed him both as President of the Association and Governor of Idaho. I had also completed the latter part of 1910 my work referred to by Charlie Woodberry. Whatever may be said of the book, it was a success from the outset.

It was adopted as a text-book in all the co-operative schools in Idaho, Washington, Oregon, Utah, California, Colorado, Nebraska and the two Dakotas, and in many other states and territories, and was read extensively by the more intelligent of the general public. Most economic works were, up to the time "Co-operative Economy" made its appearance, devoted to analysis and explanation of the competitive system. My work discussed Co-operation as it was and as it ought to be. In our schools such a work was needed, as co-operation was the chief study pursued in conjunction with all useful branches. I suppose it must be admitted that this work gives me more satisfaction at this time than anything I have ever done, because, although the Publishing department was successful under my administration, it was not due to my sole efforts. "Co-operative Economy" was my own thought and was produced outside of the work which the Association assigned me.

"Mr. Braden," said Charlie, "I would be glad to ask you a few questions about co-operation and the Co-opolitan Association if you would kindly answer them. I have a general idea of the system, but its features are not clear to my mind. If I could get in a nutshell a few truths—or what you claim to be truths—I believe I could read your books with much more interest."

"Ask me any question you please, Charlie. If I cannot answer them your sister there will," I replied.

"Charlie and I have already had some correspondence and talks on the subject," said Caroline. "He does not think the system attractive."

"I will not say it is not attractive," returned Charlie, shaking his head. "I simply say it is not attractive as I understand it. Now, take, for instance, the feature which makes the Association own everything. That is very distasteful to me. Nobody can ever own his own home, even."

"Well, Charlie," said I, "that is the way you have been educated. If you had been taught to believe that personal ownership of property was a burden, and had a tendency to diminish your personal security, you would view the case in a different light. Think a minute. Take a Mongolian when an infant, transfer him to London, rear him as a Christian and an Englishman and he will despise the system and religion of China. But take an English baby and let him be reared in Pekin as a Chinaman and he will doubtless hold London and Christianity in abhorrence.

"We talk of the peculiarities of the Chinese mind, and doubtless there are many which have been formed by the education and environments of centuries or time; but the Chinese education is more responsible for the Chinese mind than nature is.

"You have been taught that it is desirable to have property stand in your name. In the competitive system to own property makes you the object of attack. It is dangerous. You are always fearful that somebody will rob you. If you own none, in the competitive system, you are despised, no matter what your personal merits may be.

"Yet you can only use what you own and you can do no more with what you borrow.

"Why should you wish to own it, then, if you only get the use of it in any event? In the co-operative system it has been found convenient to have individuals own certain things. They own their own furniture, their clothes, wall pictures and small ornaments. In short, they own whatever in the house is severable from it, including tools which they employ for private use and what they can lightly carry about their person.

"They do not own house or grounds. They simply have the use of them. But they are entitled to the use of house, grounds and all the conveniences connected with them as long as they wish. Their children after them are entitled to that use. In the competitive system you cannot get more.

Co-operation also assumes the cares of the Co-operators as far as material things are concerned. You do not have to worry about the ownership of that which has no other than use value. In competition you have to own your property, care for it personally, protect it and pay taxes. This diverts your mind from thought and fills it with worry, and in addition to that people overlook your merit and inquire, not what you are, but what you have, and woe betide you, whatever your merit, if you have nothing."

"But does not common ownership and the inability of the occupant to own his home render him careless and wasteful? Does he take such an interest in his home as he would if he could call it his?"

"The ownership of the home in the competitive system does not make the owner so careful to avoid waste as our system makes the tenant. As I have said, the occupant, be he owner or tenant, can enjoy only the use of his house during his life.

"In the competitive system how many owners waste their houses? Some are drunkards and mortgage them and waste their value in drink. Some are gamblers, and lose the value at the gaming table. Some insure them and burn them to get the insurance money. Some go into business, mortgage the home for money or credit, fail and lose the property. Thousands of houses stand idle and go to waste in every competitive state, while thousands of homeless people walk the streets in every large city or tramp the country roads. In our system the state cares for every home and make a home for every man. The man knows his home is permanent. It cannot be taken from him without his consent."

"But he cannot convey it to his children," said Charlie.

"No. He cannot compel his children to take it whether they will or not. But if the children desire it, when the occupant dies or departs, they may have it on the same terms if they are members of the Industrial Army that their parents did. Let me say, however, that when the children marry they generally present a design of a house which suits them better than the old homestead and the Association builds them a house to suit them. Is not that better?"

"So much for the home," remarked Charlie. "I am almost satisfied with your explanation. It at least gives me the cue so that I can study the subject fully. Now, I have long felt that you were asking a man to be a slave and give up his personal liberty by entering the Industrial Army. Why is not that true?"

"Charlie, are you a slave to-day?" I asked.

"No, indeed!" exclaimed Charlie, almost indignant.

"Is a government official a **slave?**"

"Of course not."

"How about a soldier in the regular army?"

"Why, he is certainly not a slave."

"How about a clerk in the postoffice department, for instance? Is he not in the same position as a member of the Industrial Army?"

"No. It is a similar **service**, but he serves his government and country."

"What is your business, Charlie?"

"Accountant for the Waumkeag Cotton **Manufacturing** Company."

"What are your wages?"

"Eighty dollars per month."

"How many hours a day do you work?"

"Ten hours."

"Is it slavery to work ten hours a day for a private corporation, for eighty dollars per month, and not own any interest in the corporation? Remember that the Co-opolitan Association pays one hundred dollars per month and requires only seven hours' work per day at the most. Then every minute's work in the competitive system is for private persons, while in the co-operative system **it is for the public good.**"

"Well. But suppose I should want to leave the service of the Association after I had worked for it **ten** years or less. Could I withdraw my part of the accumulated wealth and take it away?"

"You could withdraw your wages and no more. You could go where you please with the wages."

"But the accumulated capital. Would it not be unjust not to let me have my part of that?"

"Charlie! I forgive you, of course, but you are brilliantly stupid. How long have you been at work for the corporation which now employs you?"

"Three years."

"If you should work for that corporation fifty years would you get any more than your wages if you should withdraw?"

"No."

"Who would get the benefit of your work?"

"Why, the stockholders."

"Yes, or perhaps the bondholders! You could invest your wages in stock in that corporation if you chose. You cannot invest them in the Association. But after investing in the cotton company you are liable to be frozen out by the big holders. Now, frankly, do you not see that you may work forty years for your company and then in old age have not enough to sustain life from day to day? This could not occur in our system. We exact now twenty-five years' work of each member and then he is free. After he has given us twenty-five years' work he becomes entitled to his dividend for the rest of his life just the same as if he worked."

"That sounds well, Mr. Braden. But have you any such retired members yet?"

"You must not call them retired members. We believe that those who earn freedom by twenty-five years' work will be among our most useful members. They will still be interested in our work. They will still participate in our elections. They will take a personal interest in maintaining and guarding the Association whence they draw their income. Our Association is now only fifteen years old. In ten years more three hundred of us will be entitled to release from systematic labor. It is possible that the Association will give us earlier release, as our co-operative wealth is so great at present, and is increasing so rapidly, that we are considering the propriety of diminishing the number of hours of labor per day to six and the number of years to twenty. We have many persons who have earned long furloughs. In every such instance the member during his or her furlough is a useful member. If he travels he brings home to us the best of information. If he seeks pleasure he studies that very important pursuit and we learn from him how to make life enjoyable."

"You certainly are able to make pertinent and seemingly complete answers, Mr. Braden. I shall ask my questions now, not to puzzle but to elicit information. Suppose a member becomes sick. Does that stop his income or dividend?"

"If a member becomes sick he is turned over to the Health department. As long as he is in the charge of the Health department his income continues."

"Who pays for his treatment by physicians?"

"He pays for it himself out of his income from the Association."

"Suppose he should wish to change his climate in order to recover? How shall he make a change?"

"If the Health department reports such a remedy for any sick member of the Industrial Army leave of absence is granted and he is permitted to go to such climate as is recommended."

"Suppose a man dies leaving a wife and family after five years' employment. What does the Association do for the family?"

"The funeral expenses are paid and the family receives the deceased member's income until the youngest child becomes of age, provided the child remains in the Educational department. If the widow is healthy and able to work she is received into the Industrial Army."

"When a man enters the Army does he become entitled to the full income of a member in good standing at once?"

"He does not. The first year he or she receives only one-third of the income of a member. The second year and all years after he receives as much as anyone. Members are on probation the first year. The three years members are entitled to promotion to higher grades and the members during the first three years are required to do the drudgery of the Association. We have made exceptions to this rule when we have offered inducements to skilled laborers, but otherwise all who enlist, especially from the Department of Education, must pass through the three years course."

"One more question, Mr. Braden, and I will ask no more until I have read some chapters of 'Co-operative Economy.' Do not your members regard a new volunteer as an intruder? Do they not consider that he is suddenly admitted to share what they have produced without making an equal contribution? You have, say, three million dollars' worth of wealth in Idaho. Why should one who never assisted in producing it be admitted to participate in its benefits without paying a large membership fee?"

"He does pay a fee of one hundred dollars and he gives the first year's labor for one-third the income of one member for that time. If he has not one hundred dollars we do not always exclude him. We simply take it out of his income. But you must remember that the Association is a great corporation, in which the shares are not transferable and one member can only own one share. The Association keeps all the machinery and sources of production in its exclusive control. Every person who enters to-day agrees to furnish twenty-five years' labor. No person can receive the benefit of such a membership unless he so agrees. The Association, therefore, has as many twenty-five-year contracts as there are members of the Industrial Army. Let us suppose that one member has worked for twenty-four years when a new member is admitted. The latter is now to work twenty-five years and the former one. The latter is to give twenty-five years' work to the former, who one year later must depend upon the labor of the latter to support him. Tell me which of these men is getting the advantage, the man whose twenty-five years of labor in the past has provided the machinery and improved the source of production or the man whose twenty-five years of the future will operate the machine and render the source of production fruitful. Is it not a fair bargain after all? If a man forty-six retires from labor and a man twenty-one takes his place and supports him will the former object?"

This closed the economic discussion. My wife did not take part except as a listener, but she was deeply interested. Our little girl had fallen asleep in her arms and she now softly arose and carried her into the sleeping apartment. Charlie and I still continued on the veranda a little longer enjoying the pure and cool atmosphere, and pursued our conversation on lighter subjects.

CHAPTER XXV.

THE TERM OF SERVICE—THE SURVIVORS OF TWENTY YEARS—SPREAD OF CO-OPERATION—SECRET OF CO-OPOLITAN SUCCESS—1917.

An important question came up before the Legislative Council at one of its meetings in May, 1916. It was as to whether the term of service in the Industrial Army should be reduced from twenty-five to twenty years.

After full discussion it was decided to refer the matter to popular vote at the referendum election of October following. It was accordingly referred, but not in the form in which it was at first considered.

The question submitted was: "Whether the term of service in the Industrial Army shall be reduced to twenty years to all members in the Grade of Honor at the expiration of that time." All persons who had performed their duties faithfully and whom their companies, by a majority vote, recommended to advancement to the Grade of Honor were, after serving fifteen years, so advanced.

This had the effect of rendering our workers more diligent, and it was believed by the members of the Legislative Council that if men could shorten their term of service five years by industry and faithfulness it would increase the efficiency of the Industrial Army. The people of Idaho thought so, too, and after a most thorough discussion, in which it was made apparent that the Association could well afford to shorten the term, the election of October resulted in a practically unanimous decision in favor of twenty years.

The 20th of May, 1917, completed the service of thirty-six members. Twenty years before our little company of fifty, under the leadership of John Thompson, had entered

Deer Valley and established our camp on the present site of Co-opolis. Since then fourteen of that company had passed to "that country from whose bourne no traveler returns." The thirty-six who remained were nearly all of them high in the councils of the Association and some had achieved reputations which extended beyond the limits of Idaho.

We who composed that little company were, on this twentieth anniversary, released from the burdens and duties attaching to the Co-opolitan system, and thenceforward were entitled to come and go at will. Wheresoever we chose a habitation in the state the Association undertook to provide us with suitable houses, and, our income continuing as large as if we were still employed, we were expected to, and could, pay the rental of the house and our living and other expenses without stint.

One dollar of credit, as represented by the labor-credit check, was neither depreciable nor appreciable by the act of interested or disinterested persons. Abundance or scarcity of any product, as measured by the demand for it, was the determining factor of price. Our credit dollar was invested with large purchasing power because co-operation produced abundance and guaranteed to each of us a quantity of any needed article, and a quality of comfort, pleasure, convenience or accommodation equal to the fair exchange value of labor.

The thirty-six whose service ceased on this anniversary were men who were devoted to the principle of co-operation and ready to make any sacrifice to the success of the Co-opolitan Association. Most of them had lived comparatively frugal lives. For fifteen years the income which they had derived from their service had been twelve hundred dollars per annum at least. This was allowed them on the books of the Association and the labor-credit checks were delivered to them each month, as to all workers. If they failed to exhaust their month's credit during the month the surplus remained with the Association.

We have no banks. We have no money and no department which makes a business of handling money. We have no occasion to deposit or store labor-credit checks.

No man has any claim with us upon anything but the fruits of labor. These we hold until he calls for them, and we pay him no interest for their use. In fact, we have no use for what he leaves with the Association. We prefer to have him take it and consume it himself. The Association, for instance, has a menagerie and circus which it sends from city to city. We see no reason why a man who desires to see such an exhibition should refrain from doing so from motives of frugality. The Association prefers that the admission fee be taken out of every labor-credit check. Of course this does not usually happen, because the members do not always desire to witness such an exhibition when it appears.

If a man is frugal and spends but little of his monthly credit he does not lose it during his life. It is a matter of prudence to save something, so that he may use it if he goes abroad, and the Association holds itself ready to furnish him the money of any nation if he makes the proper application for it.

But if a man dies his unexhausted credit is canceled. He cannot will it to his wife or children. The wife is given a place in the Industrial Army and his years of service are accredited to her; so that if he has served ten years up to the time of his death only fifteen more are required of her, or ten years if he or she should be a member of the Grade of Honor.

As for children, if they are members of the Educational department and are left orphans they are allowed the father's portion until they arrive at age, when they enter the Industrial Army. These provisions are necessary to co-operative success. To permit a man to leave his accumulations to his son or daughter takes from them the incentive to labor. They cease to be useful or acquire a superiority which nature did not give them.

We insist that all should be equal in the start, and that they have no advantages which they cannot create for themselves.

The competitor claims that this removes the incentive for action. This is not true. It removes one incentive out of many, and the worst and most injurious one.

It is an incentive which makes robbers, thieves, murderers and tyrants and produces a host of evils.

The competitor says it is unjust because it takes from wife and child their support. It does not. We give the wife a chance to be useful and an income for her use equal to the income of any.

We give the child his education and an opportunity equal to the best when he becomes a man. We insure these things, and the husband and father is relieved from all worry on their account while he lives. Is not this worth many times the riches of the competitor which are so ready to vanish and leave wife and child in the ranks of abject and despised poverty.

The twentieth year of the Co-operative Commonwealth is indeed a proud one. The great state which we occupy is entirely under the control of the Co-opolitan Association. It contains four million people and two and a half million active members of the Industrial Army. Its inhabitants are all in cities, but no city is greater than one hundred and fifty thousand persons, except Idaho Falls and Shoshone, where the great water power, generating electricity, gives exceptional advantages for manufactures. Idaho Falls contains three hundred and fifty thousand inhabitants and Shoshone two hundred and twenty-one thousand. In Shoshone are the great flouring and woolen mills, but nearly every needful and useful article is also produced through the medium of its marvelous electric power. Idaho Falls is more famous for its cotton mills, and other cities are numerous which are devoted to manufactures of various kinds. The city of Rokybar is the Pittsburg of Idaho and the Association steel works at that city are the largest in the world.

Laselle is the producer of beet sugar, and all the sugar used by our department stores in Idaho is supplied from our factories there. There is little necessity for the importation of anything into this state, so varied and abundant are its resources and productions.

These cities of Idaho are all laid out and conducted on the plan of Co-opolis. Each one of them covers an area nearly three times as large as that of any competitive city. The streets are all one hundred and fifty feet wide, consisting of two driveways fifty feet wide and a park of equal width separating them.

Numerous parks are located at convenient distances from one another. The buildings are all at least fifty feet apart. There is ample sunlight, pure air and space for children to play or for older people to take recreation.

There are flowers, fountains, artificial lakes and trees in profusion. Monuments and statues have been erected in many localities, representing art and history and illustrating the power and beauty of co-operation. The streets are all paved with asphalt. Most of our buildings are constructed of brick or stone and of the material necessary for the purpose Idaho has inexhaustible resources.

In this twentieth year of the Co-operative Commonwealth the United States is moving swiftly and quietly to that condition which Bellamy beheld in "Looking Backward." Washington was the first state to join Idaho as a Co-operative Commonwealth, which it did in 1910. Oregon, Utah, Colorado, Arizona, New Mexico, Kansas, Nebraska, North and South Dakota, Wyoming, Montana and California followed in quick succession in about the order named. Minnesota, Wisconsin, Illinois, Indiana, Michigan, Tennessee, Arkansas, North and South Carolina and Texas are almost ready to wheel into line.

As for the other states of the Union, the co-operative system is gaining ground every day. In the United States Senate there are forty Co-operative Senators. In the House of Representatives there are one hundred and forty-three Co-operators.

Through the influence of Idaho the United States government has purchased and now operates five transcontinental lines of railroad, and it is probable that it will, in a few years, acquire most of the lines which are sufficiently valuable to warrant their operation. It owns all the telegraph lines in its territory, having purchased them as early as 1908.

Nearly all the cities of the country have become the owners of their own public utilities, such as street-car lines, telephone, gas, electric and water systems and plants, and from the income derived from them have almost succeeded in relieving their citizens from the burden of taxation.

But the private department stores, labor-saving machinery, trusts and monopolies, which continue to exact tribute from and oppress the people for private gain, are our unconscious and unintentional allies, and the thousands of good citizens who yearly move westward to avail themselves of the opportunities which exist in the Co-operative Commonwealths called into being by the success of the Co-opolitan Association do not fail by their correspondence to light the fires of the new and higher civilization in every city and hamlet of the nation.

This success is one which Idaho and her people are, at this time, disposed to credit, in a somewhat larger degree than history will or should approve, to the immortal senior Senator from Idaho, Hon. John Thompson, and his associates of twenty years ago. All honor, indeed, to them!

But I maintain that conditions, circumstances and a great nation of intelligent, honest, industrious and comparatively temperate laboring men and women made their work possible in America when it could not have been successful in any other country in this world.

I do not say this from motives of patriotism. I say it because it appears to me that the reasons to support the allegation will be recognized and approved when stated.

In the first place, there has never before been any extensive experiment with industrial co-operation for the benefit of the workers engaged in it, where land was the basis of all operations, except in ancient Peru.

It is unfortunate that history has been so far deprived of the records of that wonderful country, by the destructive fanaticism of its Spanish conquerors, that the details of its system must remain obscure.

But happily the indisputable fact remains to give courage to co-operators who do battle in the dark corners of the world that Peru was a co-operative or socialistic state, and that its people were happy, prosperous and contented.

This fact suggests the very pertinent question whether the people who boast a high state of civilization like that of modern New York and Boston are equal to the establishment of a system as just, as fair and as equitable in the production, distribution and protection of wealth as the comparatively ignorant, simple-minded and uncivilized inhabitants of ancient Peru?

The example of Idaho proves that we are. But in England, France and Germany the co-operators have confined their undertakings almost exclusively to manufactures and distribution. The land has rarely entered into their calculations, or when it has been considered has never been regarded as available. In Idaho we have made land the chief feature of our enterprise, and I maintain and, in fact, know, that we could never have succeeded in any marked degree if we had not done so.

A commonwealth which has not the title to its own land is like a house suspended in the air. Even the co-operative societies engaged in manufacture and distribution manufacture and distribute what comes, primarily, from the land.

When they receive the raw material to manufacture or distribute it has been handled by a number of traders, brokers and other middlemen and its price increased oppressively. We avoided all this by owning the land.

In England and other densely populated countries the rich land has all been taken and the owner, whether lord or peasant, will not part with it except for a large sum of money. The co-operator is thus excluded, in those countries, from the use of land. It costs him nearly as much in spot cash to acquire it as the brokers and traders take from him, through a series of years, in profits on the raw product of land.

Now in Idaho land was cheap, and cheap land is the co-operator's salvation.

I also believe that we were fortunate in locating our colonies in Idaho. The reason for this is that after we had acquired the land of Deer Valley, placed it under irrigation and rendered it highly productive, we had the use of millions of acres of grazing lands for our herds and flocks.

I cannot conceive that a co-operative society could begin its career under more favorable conditions than did the Co-opolitan. It could not have found a better location for its productive farm and city in any other state. It had the best facilities for irrigation and controlling all the waters necessary to render its land productive; it had the means to attach its members to the common purpose.

It was able to avail itself of near and high-priced markets.

Better than all this, it had the open ranges embracing millions of acres of good grazing land, which it was permitted by the laws to use without cost. If we had not possessed this advantage, my judgment is that our struggle would have been increased and prolonged.

I believe that cattle and sheep were the most advantageous kind of wealth for us to handle. We allowed them to roam at will, with but few attendants, over our ranges, and we were at little expense to care for and feed them. Besides this it was a form of wealth which was capable of transporting itself to some extent. Had we attempted a different location where there were no ranges and put our capital into almost any other form of property we would have failed.

These natural advantages and the system whose development I have endeavored in these pages to trace are, in my judgment, responsible for the success which the Co-opolitan Association has made in twenty years.

L'ENVOI.

My narrative, kind reader, is finished, but if you have followed it thus far you will doubtless feel some interest in the present condition of some of its chief characters and features. Of Senator Thompson I need say only that he is one of the most honored and famous individualities in this world.

Being a native of England, he is not eligible to the Presidency of the republic, else I verily believe he would be chosen to usher in the Co-operative Commonwealth which seems to be one of the probabilities in the near future. But Senator Thompson is in the prime of manhood and you can be sure that he will be one of the chief actors in the coming change.

Mrs. Braden is, as famous in her sphere as Senator Thompson is in his. Having written, as the world knows, five novels of the highest merit, all of which have been received with extraordinary favor, the Association has rewarded her by remitting her entire term of service in the Industrial Army. This has not had the effect of silencing her muse by any means. She is as industrious as if both fame and fortune were wanting. The fires of true genius do not require the inspiration of greed to make them burn more brightly.

Mr. Edmunds is now an old man. He will accept the ease which the expiration of his term of service enables him to enjoy. Although seventy years of age, he is strong and hearty, and we hope may live, as he seems likely to, for many years.

Henry B. Henderson died three years ago. A bronze statue of him stands in the park on Commonwealth Avenue, in front of the Council Hall, and I am told that the people of Shoshone and Idaho Falls are arranging to have similar statues erected and paid for by subscription in their cities.

Boise City is a beautiful city of fifty thousand inhabitants. The municipal indebtedness of the old city was long ago purchased by the Co-opolitan Association for a small sum and the flood of co-operative enterprise poured over and through the old townsite at once.

The city of CO-OPOLIS is not, as I have already stated, the largest city in Idaho. It contains a population of one hundred and fifty thousand. It is the oldest co-operative city in the state and the most beautiful in the world. Its buildings are substantially constructed; its parks are well kept and better finished than are those of most other cities, and its trees are older and more mature. It is believed that it will be the favorite city of residence for the members whose terms of service in the Industrial Army expire. At present it is the seat of government in the Association domain.

Idaho is still a "Light on the Mountains," as its ancient name implies, and its effulgence had found a shining way into thousands of homes throughout the world.

Truly may it be said that her mission is being grandly accomplished and that the people that dwelt in darkness have seen a great light.

Thank God! The higher civilization is here.

[THE END.]

THE SOCIAL DEMOCRACY OE AMERICA

has as one of its main objects the peaceable establishment, in some such manner as outlined in this book, of the

CO-OPERATIVE COMMONWEALTH.

We believe in the efficacy of object lessons, and the Social Democracy of America is working for and advocating the Co-operative Commonwealth, where all shall receive their full share of the wealth they create and the Brotherhood of Man shall be an actual fact. In order to do its work in establishing this ideal state of perfect justice between man and man the

COLONIZATION COMMISSION

of the Social Democracy of America has formulated plans and methods for putting the ideas contained in this book into actual operation.

If one million working men would pay ten cents each into a fund to help such a plan, it would mean one hundred thousand dollars a month, or one million two hundred thousand dollars a year. If one hundred thousand should do so, it would mean one thousand dollars a month and one hundred and twenty thousand dollars a year. In five years, with judicious management and cautions expenditure of such funds, the results would be marvelous, especially as a dollar in the hands of co-operators would prove far more efficient than a dollar employed in the extravagant and wasteful channels of competition.

Send a dollar for thirty-four sample copies and make thirty-four converts to the cause of reform.

Six cents will pay for "Merrie England," a book of 190 pages, which has had a sale of 850,000 copies in England and has only begun to sell in America. It is a popular yet scientific statement of the principles of Socialism. It is addressed to the people who are prejudiced against anything of the kind. Get a man to read "Merrie England" and the book will do the rest. We mail two copies for 10 cents, twelve for 50 cents, twenty-five for $1.00, a hundred for $3.50.

Ten cents will pay for "President John Smith," by Frederick Upham Adams, a book of 300 pages. It has passed through twenty-five editions in a year. It is a success because it points out practical methods for intelligent political action by which the people of the United States may take possession of the government and run it in their own interest. We mail a dozen copies for $1.00; fifty copies for $3.75.

Twenty-five cents will pay for any one of the following valuable books:

The Co-opolitan, by Zebina Forbush.
Evolutionary Politics, by Walter Thomas Mills.
Man or Dollar, Which? by a newspaper man.
From Earth's Center, by S. Byron Welcome.
A Breed of Barren Metal, by J. W. Bennett.
Money Found, by Thomas E. Hill.

The six books, or six copies of any one of them, will be sent postpaid on receipt of one dollar. Special terms to agents, with full list of reform literature, will be mailed upon request.

Address
CHARLES H. KERR & COMPANY, Publishers,
56 Fifth Avenue, Chicago.

MEN WANTED.

We firmly believe that in "The Co-opolitan" we are giving to the people of the United States a book that will be of untold value in hastening the progress of human brotherhood and a civilization based on justice. We believe the people are ready for this book, and that any intelligent man who believes in co-operation and knows how to express his ideas can make a good living by selling copies. We want to hear from such men.

We also want to hear from those who have no time for selling books but who believe intensely in human brotherhood and want to do their part in making it a fact in this present life. Our object is to provide them with literature for wide distribution, at prices that are based on the actual cost of production.

One cent will pay for a copy of "The Ethical Aspect of the Labor Problem," by Rev. J. Stitt Wilson. It is addressed to Christians and proves that the profit system under which the people are struggling is directly opposed to the teachings of Jesus.

Two cents will pay for "The New Democracy," by Frederick Upham Adams, the editor of The New Time. It is a clear and forceful statement of the ideas of Direct Legislation through the Initiative and Referendum.

Three cents will pay for a new pamphlet entitled "The Majority Rule League of the United States," which gives a practical plan for organization to be put in practice at once. It gives a valuable appendix on Direct Legislation. Fifty copies mailed for $1.00; 500 for $7.50.

Three cents will pay for a sample copy of The New Time, the greatest reform magazine in the world, 100 large pages each month, full of timely articles, news and pictures that no reformer will consent to do without if he once sees it.

The three members of the commission were appointed August 1, 1897, and their work was outlined before the publication of this book.

The manuscript was read by one of the members of the commission and received his hearty commendation, as presenting arguments of a high character in favor of colonization. Many ideas elucidating legal points are also brought out in the clearest manner.

The Commission is attempting to work out practically the main idea presented in this book. Any reader who becomes desirous of aiding in this noble work, or who wishes information concerning it, should address Secretary Colonization Commission, S. D. of A.,

504 Trude Bldg.,
Chicago, Ill.

THE LEGAL REVOLUTION OF 1902.

BY
A LAW-ABIDING REVOLUTIONIST.

CHICAGO:
CHARLES H. KERR & COMPANY.
1898.

The following specimen pages of
"THE LEGAL REVOLUTION OF 1902"
are published by permission of the author from advance proofs of the book, which is now in press. Every loyal reformer will be interested in this new work, which outlines a radical and aggressive political programme to be carried out in the near future. The book will be handsomely printed on heavy book paper of extra quality, and will be sold at fifty cents in paper and one dollar in cloth, with liberal terms to dealers, agents and newspapers.

PREFACE.

"The Legal Revolution of 1902" purports to be a history of social conditions in the United States for a period of about fifteen years following the year 1897. It attempts to picture changes and reforms amounting to an industrial revolution—which I think should, and will, be made—as if the country had already passed through this period. All matters of fact recorded as having taken place before 1897, or "before the Revolution," are true; quotations from newspapers and other publications, and utterances of men, prior to that year, are also true; whatever is mentioned as occurring afterward is, of course, fiction.

Some of the characters in this narrative bear the same names as distinguished persons of to-day, but no pretense nor claim is made that they speak or represent in any manner the views or sentiments of those whose names they may happen to bear. The characters have been named to give added interest to the story, to connect it more plainly with the evident trend of social and political conditions, and to more clearly elucidate the opportunities which lie within the power of men.

The principal idea of the work is to show the people their power, wherein it lies, and the methods of exercising it to right their grievances, if they feel that such exist.

If I succeed in bringing all who read these pages to a full understanding of the power of the people, and how to use that power, and wherein lies the basis, the very foundation, of our institutions, I shall be content, even though they do not agree with this story as to the extent of existing evils, or the measures it inaugurates to alleviate them. While endeavoring to clothe my ideas in an interesting and readable narrative, some exaggerations have been made; yet, in confidence to the reader, it must be said that, in the main, I believe in every line of the work; in the principle of every reform proposed; in every change pictured and result prophesied. Indeed, I can see no other road for a law-abiding, intelligent and prosperous people to travel, and no other possible destination to be reached, than the one herein imperfectly portrayed.

A LAW-ABIDING REVOLUTIONIST.

THE LEGAL REVOLUTION OF 1902.

CHAPTER I.

"Well, mother, I'll run down and get the mail," said John Brown to his wife, as he started for the village post-office. On arriving there he found his "grist" of daily papers that regularly visited his home, and also two letters. One was addressed "Hon. John Brown, Member of the Illinois Legislature." He looked at it and incidentally remarked to a friend with whom he was conversing: "I wonder who that is from—'Return in five days to Mark Mishler, Attorney-at-Law, Springfield, Ill.'; I guess it is not of much importance to me; I don't know any such person." And with that he put it, unopened, into his pocket, and looked at the other.

"Indeed, New York, from brother Benjamin! I haven't heard from him in a long time. Mother and I were just talking about him and wondering if he had forgotten us. She'll want to hear the news, and I had better go right back to the house," and he started, carrying the letter and papers in his hand. It was but a few minutes' walk, and he was soon home.

"See here, mother, a letter from Ben," he said, starting to tear it open.

"Is it possible!" she exclaimed, with considerable surprise; "we haven't heard from him since his wife died. He is no hand to write, and I'll warrant it is news of importance; probably sad news, or we wouldn't hear from him now. You remember he never wrote us that Glen (his only child) was born until he was two years old. Of course he wrote during that time, but never mentioned that fact, and it was so strange, since he always writes so much about him now, when he writes at all."

By this time the letter was opened, the spectacles adjusted to his nose, and Mr. Brown began to read:

"My Dear Brother and Sister—

"You know how difficult it is for me to write, and I am sure you won't think strange because of not having heard from me before. I often think of you both, and have frequently resolved to write, but have neglected it until days, weeks and months have slipped away. I am in deep trouble now. You know that ten years ago the company set me back to flagman. The wages for such a position are very low; I have been able only to live and keep the family, and have found it impossible to lay by anything. A year ago an accident, a collision, occurred in the yards between a couple of switching freight trains. It was charged to me and I was 'laid off.' Perhaps I was to blame. I worked long hours and was very tired. I am getting old, anyway. My eyes, and faculties as well, are getting dim. Since then I have had no work, and have employed my time about the garden and with my poultry, out of which I have made a little.

"But Glen, though only sixteen, had completed school, and had also learned the glassblower's trade in the factory here, and with my pension and what little I could earn was able to support me and keep the house up in good shape, so I did not feel badly. In my old age I felt I had earned a rest; and Glen, noble boy! was satisfied, and insisted that I should have it. But now, just as he has his trade well learned, and had, as we supposed, the means of gaining a livelihood through life for himself and a way of supporting me in my old age, improved machines were introduced into many of the larger factories, that almost entirely displaced the glassblower and absolutely ruined his trade. They were not put in the factory here, but it was seen that the factory would be unable to compete with the machine-equipped factories, and that they must put them in or close up.

"After the machines began to be used it was evident that half the factories would supply the market. So the big ones all joined together into one big company, or trust, and closed up a number of the factories. The one here went into the big company, and the Board of Directors of the big concern voted it to be one of the factories that would be permanently closed. Lots of the machinery has been moved away, and there is little probability of it ever being operated again. At any rate it has now been closed for three months, and Glen has been unable to find a day's work of any kind to do, and there is little hope of any here. Glassblowers have been laid off in all the factories that are still running, and those now retained are taken from the force of older employes and there is no chance whatever for a new man now. So Glen will probably never find work again at his trade.

"And the town! You have no idea of the condition here. The glass factory was almost the sole industry. There is not another enterprise of any importance. Two thousand men, who fed ten thousand people, or the whole town, are thrown out of employment at the mandate of a trust, and the whole place is ruined. No western cyclone ever wrought worse havoc, because after one of them has passed the people can go to work and rebuild, but there is nothing here they can do to get even bread to eat.

"The very day it was known the factory would be permanently closed residence property depreciated one-half, and in fact it is scarcely worth anything now, and will not sell at any price. My place, which cost me a lifetime of toil, and for which I paid $2,500 principal and no end of interest, will not sell to-day for $500.

"But the question with the people here is, not how

much their property has depreciated in value, but how they are to get work by which to earn a living.

"Glen and I think we want to go West. We would like to go out where you are, and want to know what you think about it. Can we make a living there? We have been thinking if we could get a little patch of ground near some good-sized town we could, by gardening and poultry raising (at which I am becoming expert, by the way), get along and make a living; and Glen is a bright scholar, and I have been thinking that perhaps he could get work of some kind out there.

"I don't want to be a burden on you, but God knows I will be on the state if things continue as they are. And Glen, he deserves a better fate than the world seems to have allotted him.

"Please let me hear from you soon. With kind regards to sister Jane and yourself,

"I am, your brother,
 "BENJAMIN BROWN."

Mr. Brown was visibly affected as he slowly read the letter, and tears filled the eyes of both himself and his wife by the time it was completed.

"Well, mother, what had I better write him?"

To which the good woman quickly replied: "Send for them both to come at once and make their home with us—at least for the present. You will soon go to Springfield, and will be gone all winter attending the Legislature. You expect to hire someone to attend the stock and the farm while you are away, and you always hire in the summer. Perhaps they might like farm work, and suit you better than anyone you can hire, and so stay permanently.

"The Lord has taken all our dear children away," she continued; "and if Glen is the boy his father has always

" 'Fellow reformers, would you be **free?** Would you see the regimen of corporate power and class despotism at an end? Would you see the shackles stricken forever from the limbs **of humanity,** and behold emancipation— the rebirth? Do you **believe** that **this can** come through **the** ballot? No! You do **not.**

" 'Have not the reformers spent their lives, their fortunes, and their energies in the cause of political reform? Have they not seen the cunning and unscrupulous always victorious, emerging from every campaign master of the spoils? Have you any hopes that this will be changed in the future? The past is one long protest against the ballot as an instrument of reformation.'

"Scarcely a day passes that I do not receive one or more appeals to join one or the other of the revolutionary orders being formed in this country, and offers of money and arms are frequently received if I will give my efforts to the **cause** of revolution. Thus far I have persistently declined to give aid or encouragement to such movements. But if, through the writings of such men as Private Dalzell, revolution comes, in spite of all efforts to prevent it, I will not be found among the cowards, nor on the side of the plutocratic classes. * * *

"J. R. SOVEREIGN."

"Let me see your scrap-book, please," said Glen. It was handed to him, and he settled down to read, while the others conversed.

"That letter appeared some time ago," said Benjamin, "and I'll warrant it has been read by every member of a labor union. I tell you something is going to happen. Where, or when, **or** what it is going to be I don't know, but I do know the power of the labor unions, and doubt not they will play **an** important **part in** the struggle. I haven't a particle of doubt but those societies which Mr. Sovereign mentions are being formed. It is this great chasm between the rich and the poor that is causing the trouble. The laboring people are piling up wealth, and it is all being appropriated by the rich, and the poor find it harder each day to make a living. This is especially true in the factories of the East, where labor-saving machines are displacing thousands of laborers."

"Don't you think," said Mr. Smith, "that their further introduction should be prohibited?"

"The labor unions," was the reply, "do now, to some extent. The shoe manufacturers of Lynn have not dared to introduce a certain lasting machine recently invented, because the lasters' union has declared against it, and yet it is claimed that that machine will revolutionize the shoe business. You see that shows the strength of the unions, and what they can do if they get started. Oh, there are bloody times ahead for us. I believe one of your Western governors said lately: 'The high buildings and grand palaces of our big cities will be spattered with the lungs and livers of humanity before this thing is adjusted.' He was called a crank, but he was not far amiss."

"I am inclined to think," said Mr. Smith, "that you take a too serious view of matters. Your brother tells me the glass factory in your town was permanently closed by a trust. Is that possible? I never heard of such an outrage. I should think the managers of the trusts would be in danger of their lives."

"Now you are coming to it. See! it makes a revolutionist out of you to even hear of such a thing," said Benjamin; "yet you don't see revolution coming. Suppose you knew nothing but one trade, and you found the factory in which you had worked all your life permanently closed by a trust, and it was impossible to ever again work at your trade. When you become an actor in such an affair it is worse than a picture in your imagination. If you were placed in that position you would see what is coming."

"But has it really been permanently closed by the trust?" he again asked.

"Closed! Why, certainly, and it is nothing new. Hundreds of factories have been permanently shut down by trusts, in order to decrease production, raise prices and throw thousands of laborers out of work."

"Well," said Mr. Smith, "I guess you are right, but what is it going to be, and what are they going to do?"

"O, I don't know. They will at least have revenge. It may be we'll have anarchy, and the fulfillment of the bloody scenes painted in that wonderful book, 'Caesar's Column.' Have you read it? It is fearful. Enough to curdle a man's blood."

At this point Glen, who was still looking over his uncle's scrap-book, said: "I believe Uncle John is getting to be quite a Socialist, judging from these clippings. Let me read some of them. They are mostly from the metropolitan dailies":

"WANT IN THE CITIES.

"A few days ago we quoted from an editorial in the New York Tribune to show that there never before was such great distress in the chief city in the country as at present, and that the victims were not merely laboring men, unable to find employment, but professional people and small merchants as well. The Times-Herald editorially testifies that want is as general and intense in Chicago as in New York. It says:

" 'Perhaps since the great fire there has not been a keener occasion for generous giving. The country is now in the fourth year of a period of hard times. Very rich men have had their fortunes trimmed, so to speak; moderately rich men have been reduced to a sharp counting of the cost of casual luxuries. All classes have suffered in degree, but thousands and thousands of those brave folks whose only hope in life is to fight for the ship till they fall face forward fighting on the deck have been precipitated from a hard-earned and perilous independence into a black and hopeless poverty. * * * We do not share the opinion of the versifier who wrote "Organized charity, cold as ice, in the name of a hard, statistical Christ," but we submit that the present crisis, when ill-clad, half-famished shapes confront us on the streets; when the cold pinches the denizens of hovels and tenements; when the children in a thousand squalid homes cry for sustenance, when women fight for bread at the county agent's door, and able-bodied men swarm on the railroad tracks, eagerly begging fragments of coal—this crisis is not to be met with perfunctory measures.'

"In another article published in its news columns the Times-Herald declares that:

" 'Chicago has 8,000 families actually starving to death.

" 'It has 40,000 wives, husbands and children begging for a pittance of food to keep body and soul together—huddled into single rooms and freezing in the blizzard that visited the city yesterday.' "

The next item reads:

"DISTRESS IN GREAT CITIES.

"The public authorities and organized charities of Chicago are having more than they can do to care for the tens of thousands of destitute people in the Garden City, and the New York Tribune confesses that the want in that town is as dire as in Chicago. 'At no moment within the memory of the present generation,' says the Tribune, 'has the number of unemployed in this city been so large as just now, and never before has the strain on public and private charity been so severe as during this winter season (1896-97). It is not merely the laboring classes—that is to say, the classes who may be regarded as within facile reach of philanthropic relief—who are the sufferers, but those who may be described as professional men, clerks, the salesmen, the architects and the literary men. Few, save the clergy and physicians, have any idea of the extent to which privation and actual want prevail among these victims of the bad times that are marking the close of the deplorable Democratic administration, and doctor and parson alike wax eloquent about the destitution of the families of those unfortunate men who, while eager for work and ready to do anything for the sake of a living, are for the first time in their lives unable to find employment of any kind.' After adverting to the sympathy extended to the unfortunate inmates of Sing Sing and other prisons, who are losing their sanity because there is no work to employ them, the Tribune adds: 'It may be questioned whether the first duty of the people of New York is not toward those of their more honest and honorable fellow-citizens whose enforced idleness, due to their inability to find any employment, is driving them, too, to the verge of insanity—an insanity caused not so much by the brooding over their own unhappy lot as by the spectacle of their wives and little ones literally starving before their eyes. It is not merely on the ground of philanthropy and charity that some means or other should be devised for their relief, but on the score of policy and economy. For the less enforced idleness there is outside the prison the fewer convicts there will be within its walls.'"

The next clipping is as follows:

CHAPTER II.

In November, 1897, when evil forebodings were everywhere hovering about, Mark Mishler, a robust, big-hearted, good-natured lawyer, sat one day in his office at Springfield, Ill. He had just been beaten in a case he had tried before the Supreme Court because the law on which he based the case was declared by the Court to be unconstitutional. He never was mad; his good soul would not let him; but if ever he was perplexed it was now. His mind reverted to the Constitution of the State. He read it over, as he had done many times before, but now he took a special interest in reviewing it. As he read and reread he said to himself: "Thank God! There is one thing bigger than a Court—that is the Constitution, and the people are above that yet. They make the Constitution itself. It ought to have more laws embodied in it, and this one should have been a part of it."

And as he thought on his mind reverted to the Constitution of the United States. He turned to it and scanned it over for the first time in many years, perhaps since he was a law student. He had little practice in the United States Courts, and had had no occasion to read it. After he had finished he leaned back in his chair in a meditative mood, saying to himself: "There is the foundation of all our institutions, State and National. That was the beginning. It was the corner-stone of the Republic, and on it all that is good in this country is based."

THE LEGAL REVOLUTION OF 1902

He thought on, and added to himself: "And all that is evil, then, must likewise find its basis there."

The very thought surprised him. In deep meditation, and with strange, unaccountable feelings, he continued until he read the article recognizing human slavery, and declaring the slave trade should not be prohibited before the year 1808. He always knew that, yet he could hardly believe his eyes. He read on till he came to the amendment freeing the slaves, adopted nearly three-quarters of a century afterward.

"Well," he gasped, almost aloud, "I knew that; I helped pass that very amendment freeing the slaves and, as we were charged at the time, 'confiscating millions of dollars' worth of property.' But lawyer as I am, with twenty-five years of practice, I never thought but Lincoln's proclamation freed the slaves."

He dropped back in his chair, lost for half an hour in silent study. As he sat, entirely consumed in his own thought, his very countenance unconsciously brightened. His heart grew light. His eyes beamed within him. He felt a sort of inspiration. A new idea, and a happy one indeed, sprang like an angel of light into his mind.

He well knew, and had studied much, of the rise and fall of the grand ancient civilizations, and with evil forebodings hovering like a dark, dreary, dangerous cloud over our land, he had often pondered long as to what would be the outcome with this one. As he went to and from his office and his home, and each day met men strong, hearty, but pale-faced, asking, not for bread, but in the name of God for work, he could not well prevent the question recurring to his mind. He had often thought the last star of hope for our civilization had almost set, but as he sat there that moment, in all-absorbing thought, behind a suddenly beaming countenance, all those evil forecasts left him. Our civilization would live! The sad pictures of strikes, riots, war, famine, and pestilence, and a constantly decaying civilization, were no longer stern realities. It was like being awakened from an ugly nightmare by the sweet chipper of the birds on a bright spring morning, with the beautiful rays of the rising sun streaming through his windows.

He had seen, as by a flashlight, the people's great highway to peace, to prosperity, and to happiness. He saw wherein lay the power, the strength, of the people. The ballot was indeed all-powerful. When properly applied it was above and beyond Congress and Courts. It was the Legislature that made laws for legislatures. It was the Court of Courts, and from its decision there was no appeal. He had read again, for the first time in years, the article (No. V.) in the United States Constitution providing for its amendment, and for a Constitutional convention. Through the United States Constitutional convention the people's will was law, upon which no court could pass judgment, even if their law provided that the Court itself be abolished and the judges retired to private life without salary or with the additional penalty that they be transported. Anything the people wanted they might have. What more could they ask or hope for by resorting to riot and war? How many of the people knew this? Practically none of them.

Mark Mishler then and there declared to himself that

www.ingramcontent.com/pod-product-compliance
Lightning Source LLC
Chambersburg PA
CBHW020845160426
43192CB00007B/796